A New Approach to Conventional Arms Control in Europe

Addressing the Security Challenges of the 21st Century

SAMUEL CHARAP, ALICE LYNCH, JOHN J. DRENNAN,
DARA MASSICOT, GIACOMO PERSI PAOLI

RAND NATIONAL SECURITY RESEARCH DIVISION

For more information on this publication, visit www.rand.org/t/RR4346

Library of Congress Cataloging-in-Publication Data is available for this publication.
ISBN: 978-1-9774-0445-9

Published by the RAND Corporation, Santa Monica, Calif.

Cover: U.S. Army hosting a Russian Vienna Document inspection team to observe exercise Saber Guardian at Novo Selo Training Area, Bulgaria, 2017 (U.S. Army photo).

Preface

Conventional arms control has played a historic role in ensuring the security of Europe and the broader Euro-Atlantic region. Nearly three decades after the signing of the Treaty on Conventional Armed Forces in Europe (CFE), however, the European conventional arms control regime is moribund. Even if the political disputes that played a central role in undermining the CFE treaty could be resolved, there would be no strategic logic in reviving it. Indeed, the rationale for the CFE treaty—addressing a destabilizing quantity of conventional arms on the European continent—is no longer relevant today. In short, there is no existing framework for producing a conventional arms control agreement that could address current security challenges. With support from the German Federal Foreign Office, the RAND Corporation sought to identify such a framework. The results are presented in this report.

This project was conducted in the International Security and Defense Policy Center (ISDP) of RAND's National Security Research Division (NSRD). NSRD conducts research and analysis for the Office of the Secretary of Defense, the Joint Staff, the Unified Combatant Commands, the defense agencies, the Navy, the Marine Corps, the U.S. Coast Guard, the U.S. Intelligence Community, allied foreign governments, and foundations. For more information on the RAND International Security and Defense Policy Center, see www.rand.org/nsrd/ndri/centers/isdp or contact the center director (contact information is provided on the webpage).

Contents

Figures and Tables

Figures

Tables

Summary

Conventional arms control (CAC) has played a historic role in ensuring the security of Europe and the broader Euro-Atlantic region. It was a crucial element of the multilevel negotiations that ended the Cold War peacefully. Signed in 1990, the Treaty on Conventional Armed Forces in Europe (CFE) made a significant contribution to stability on the continent at a time of dramatic change. By establishing ceilings on categories of arms that were believed to facilitate a large-scale surprise attack and creating procedures for inspection and notification, CFE fostered stability—not only in the final years of the Cold War, but also during the early post–Cold War period, when hundreds of thousands of troops and their materiel were moving across the continent. CFE was augmented by the other two components of the broader European CAC regime: the Vienna Document (VDoc), a set of regional confidence and security-building measures (CSBMs), and the Open Skies Treaty (OST), which allows for aerial reconnaissance flights.

Today, however, the CAC regime has largely collapsed. Russia suspended implementation of CFE in 2007.[1] North Atlantic Treaty Organization (NATO) states-parties to the treaty, along with Georgia and Moldova, retaliated by ceasing to implement their CFE obligations vis-à-vis Russia in 2011. Meanwhile, the Agreement on Adaptation of CFE (A/CFE), an update of the original treaty signed in 1999, never entered into force and there is no realistic prospect of it ever doing so. Today, CFE implementation continues in a vestigial fashion,

[1] It should be noted that there is no provision in the CFE treaty for suspending its implementation.

but its impact on the security environment is negligible. Disputes surrounding OST implementation seem to threaten its continuing viability, with persistent press reporting in late 2019 about a possible U.S. withdrawal from the treaty.[2] VDoc implementation is less contested, but efforts to modernize the agreement to make it relevant to current security challenges have repeatedly failed.

Observers on all sides are extremely pessimistic about the short-term prospects for reviving the CAC regime in its current form. The scholar Łukasz Kulesa has noted that the existing regimes are "so contested and compromised that they are no longer feasible bases for an effective new system."[3] Yet even if the political disputes surrounding the CAC regime were to be resolved, today there would be no strategic logic in reviving its central pillar, CFE or A/CFE. The rationale for the CFE treaty—addressing a destabilizing quantity of conventional arms on the European continent—is no longer relevant in 2020. Today, large numbers of CFE-limited equipment are clearly no longer the primary threat, and quantity is no longer commensurate with capabilities in light of military-technological developments since the original treaty was negotiated. In short, there is no existing framework for producing a conventional arms control agreement relevant to current security challenges. This report aims to help identify such a framework by asking first-order questions about the military drivers of potential conflict and using the answers to suggest a menu of possible CAC measures to address those drivers.

---

[2] Michael R. Gordon and Vivian Salama, "Trump Moves Closer to Ending Another Post-Cold War Treaty," *Wall Street Journal*, October 27, 2019.

[3] Łukasz Kulesa, "The Future of Conventional Arms Control in Europe," *Survival*, Vol. 60, No. 4, 2018, p. 80.

Research Approach

This study focused exclusively on addressing potential conflict involving NATO member states and Russia (and its ally Belarus);[4] we did not seek to devise CAC solutions to the other major security challenges in Europe, such as the protracted conflicts in the South Caucasus or in Ukraine.

To design CAC measures relevant for current security challenges, this report examines the potential military-driven causes of conflict between Russia and NATO, specifically those that such measures could plausibly address. It does so using two different sets of inputs: an analysis of threat perceptions of several of the key states involved, and an examination of conflict scenarios involving Russia and NATO. We deliberately excluded those drivers of conflict that a CAC regime could not address, such as deliberate, intentional aggression or nuclear weapons. In addition to the conventional military drivers of conflict, we also sought to address escalation in the early stages of such a potential conflict.

The threat-perceptions research and scenario-building exercise provided a variety of data on the potential causes of conflict between Russia and NATO. We broke these data down into specific events on the road to war; in other words, specific escalatory actions that precipitate conflict. These events, in turn, were further disaggregated into what we termed *military factors*: generalizable categories for military dynamics that had an escalatory effect. Ultimately, we identified 14 such factors. We then sought to devise CAC measures to address these factors, using findings from a workshop, original research, and studies conducted during the CFE and A/CFE negotiating periods.

---

[4] Of Russia's allies in the Collective Security Treaty Organization, Belarus is the only one geographically relevant to potential Russia-NATO conflict.

Findings

The findings of the study are presented below in the form of a catalogue of the 14 military factors identified as the key drivers of potential NATO-Russia conflict and escalation, with the CAC measures to address them listed below each factor. This is a menu of possible measures to consider, not a proto-treaty or proposal. Detailed descriptions of each factor and measure can be found in Chapters Four and Five, respectively.

Table S.1
Military Factors and Potential Conventional Arms Control Measures to Address Them

Military Factor	Potential Conventional Arms Control Measures to Address Factor
1. Military activities, including deployments, in strategically sensitive locations	a. Limitations on permanently based forces and infrastructure (including storage sites) in the designated sensitive locations. i. Limits on the types of units or numbers of certain units permitted to be permanently based in sensitive locations. b. Bans or limits on permanent deployments of enablers required for surprise attack, such as tactical fuelers, air defense, combat bridges, or electronic warfare capabilities, within the zone. c. Restrictions on colocation of enablers and related capabilities that are required for surprise attack or cross-border operations within the zone. d. Limitations on codeployment of certain units to minimize offensive capability of permanently stationed forces within the zone. e. Limitations on size of temporary additional deployments in sensitive locations. f. Rather than limitations, a measure could consist of commitments regarding the size or nature of potential future deployments in the sensitive area. g. Limitations on out-of-garrison activities of permanently stationed forces within the sensitive area. h. Notification-threshold requirements for deployments or other activities in sensitive locations. i. Enhanced information exchanges on forces permanently stationed within the specified area.
2. Military activities, including deployments, involving new or escalatory capabilities in strategically sensitive locations	a. Bans or limits on deployments of specified capabilities in designated sensitive areas, except in the context of notified exercises. b. Notification requirements for deployments of specified capabilities or activities involving specified capabilities in sensitive locations.

Table S.1—Continued

Military Factor	Potential Conventional Arms Control Measures to Address Factor
3. Training exercises in strategically sensitive locations	a. Ban or limit on number of exercises in sensitive locations. b. Limit on size of exercises in sensitive locations. c. Limit on duration of exercises in sensitive locations. d. Ban or limit on number of no-notice exercises in sensitive locations. e. Limit on the size of no-notice exercises in sensitive locations. f. Limit on total number of troops involved in parallel exercises in sensitive zones. g. Establishment of a minimum time period between single exercises in sensitive locations. h. No threshold for observation and notification of exercises in sensitive locations. i. Additional provisions for naval exercise observation and notification in sensitive zones. j. Limitations or voluntary commitments on the number of naval vessels participating in joint maritime-land-air exercises within the zone.
4. Training exercises involving new or escalatory capabilities in strategically sensitive locations	a. Limit on which capabilities can be used in exercises in strategically sensitive locations.
5. Training exercises involving the use of live force in the maritime domain	a. Live-fire exercises limited to pre-agreed naval ranges. b. Enhanced notification or observation requirements for naval exercises involving live fire.
6. Enhanced readiness	a. Agreed definitions of "readiness" and regular exchange of additional data. b. Notification mechanisms for enhanced readiness of forces. i. Prior notification could be required for moving units not designated as high-readiness to such a state. ii. Temporary deployment of those units designated as high-readiness could be subject to advance notification. c. Limitations on overall readiness. d. Notification requirements for movements of high-readiness forces.

Table S.1—Continued

Military Factor	Potential Conventional Arms Control Measures to Address Factor
7. Massing of forces	a. Regular information exchange on deployments. b. Measures to prevent concentration of forces along borders. c. Notification of plans to mass forces. d. Measures to complicate rapid concentration of forces. i. A cap on the number of assembled railcars in any one railyard. ii. Limitations on permanent fuel storage at dispersal airfields and notification requirements before establishing temporary fuel storage at such airfields. iii. Notification period before assembling more than four roll-on/roll-off ships and more than four break-bulk ships. e. Limitation on number of units that can be out of garrison at any time.
8. Violations of airspace (or perceived violations)	a. Creation of Nuclear Risk Reduction Center (NRRC)–like nodes for crisis communications. b. Creation of a special standing consultative body to address incidents. c. Creation of an updated, multilateral Prevention of Dangerous Military Activities agreement (PDMA).
9. Violations of maritime borders (or perceived violations)	a. Creation of NRRC-like nodes for crisis communications. b. Creation of a special standing consultative body to address incidents. c. Establish standalone, multilateral NATO-Russia Incidents at Sea Agreement.
10. Proximity of forces or capabilities that reduces decisionmaking time	a. Measure to ensure that naval vessels maintain a certain distance. b. Measures that fall under Factor 1 would likely address proximity in the land domain.
11. Long-range strike deployment that puts sensitive areas at risk	a. Numerical ceilings on holdings of long-range precision-guided munitions (PGMs). b. Geographical restrictions on deployment of long-range strike capabilities. c. Measures that increase time needed to strike. d. Regular declarations regarding PGMs. e. Notification requirements specific to PGMs.

Table S.1—Continued

Military Factor	Potential Conventional Arms Control Measures to Address Factor
12. Threats to vulnerable lines of communication	a. For the land domain, the vulnerability of lines of communication could be reduced by designing the sensitive zones around them.
13. Ambiguous incident	a. Creation of NRRC-style communication nodes among all relevant states. b. Creation of an updated, multilateral PDMA.
14. Lack of transparency regarding capabilities	a. Obligatory demonstration procedures for new weapon systems. b. Updated OST or persistent shared surveillance.

Acknowledgments

The authors would like to thank the German Federal Foreign Office for sponsoring this project. Additionally, we are grateful to BG (ret.) Gregory Govan and Lt Gen (ret.) Frank Klotz for their insightful reviews of the manuscript. The authors alone, however, bear responsibility for the report's contents.

Abbreviations

A2/AD	anti-access/area denial
A/CFE	Agreement on Adaptation of the Treaty on Conventional Armed Forces in Europe
APS	Army prepositioned stocks
BMD	ballistic missile defense
C2	command and control
CAC	conventional arms control
CFE	Treaty on Conventional Armed Forces in Europe
CSBM	confidence and security-building measures
eFP	enhanced forward presence
EW	electronic warfare
IADS	integrated air defenses
INCSEA	Incidents at Sea Agreement
INF	Intermediate-Range Nuclear Forces Treaty
IPW	initial period of war
LoC	line of communication
LRS	long-range strike

NATO	North Atlantic Treaty Organization
NRRC	Nuclear Risk Reduction Center
OSCE	Organization for Security and Co-operation in Europe
OST	Open Skies Treaty
PDMA	Prevention of Dangerous Military Activities agreement
PGM	precision-guided munition
SLCM	sea-launched cruise missile
SSBN	nuclear-powered ballistic missile submarine
UAV	unmanned aerial vehicle
VDoc	Vienna Document

CHAPTER ONE

Introduction

Conventional arms control (CAC) has played a historic role in ensuring the security of Europe and the broader Euro-Atlantic region. It was a crucial element of the multilevel negotiations that ended the Cold War peacefully. Signed in 1990, the Treaty on Conventional Armed Forces in Europe (CFE) made a significant contribution to stability on the continent at a time of dramatic change. By establishing ceilings on categories of arms that were believed to facilitate a large-scale surprise attack and creating procedures for inspection and notification, CFE fostered stability—not only in the final years of the Cold War, but also during the early post–Cold War period, when hundreds of thousands of troops and their materiel were moving across the continent. All told, 72,000 pieces of Cold War military equipment were eliminated under CFE's auspices.[1] CFE was augmented by the other two components of the broader European CAC regime: the Vienna Document (VDoc), a set of regional confidence and security-building measures (CSBMs), and the Open Skies Treaty (OST), which allows for aerial reconnaissance flights.

Today, however, the CAC regime has largely collapsed. Russia suspended implementation of CFE in 2007.[2] North Atlantic Treaty Organization (NATO) states-parties to the treaty, along with Georgia and Moldova, retaliated by ceasing to implement their CFE obliga-

[1] Rose Gottemoeller, "Revitalizing Security Cooperation in Europe," speech delivered at the Moscow Conference on International Security, Moscow, Russia, May 23, 2013.

[2] It should be noted that there is no provision in the CFE treaty for suspending its implementation.

tions vis-à-vis Russia in 2011. Meanwhile, the Agreement on Adaptation of CFE (A/CFE), an update of the original treaty that was signed in 1999, never entered into force and there is no realistic prospect of it ever doing so. Today, CFE implementation continues in a vestigial fashion—for example, Canadian troops inspected Belarus in January 2017, and Belarus did the same in Poland in May 2017—but its impact on the security environment is negligible. Disputes surrounding OST implementation seem to threaten its continuing viability, with persistent press reporting in late 2019 about a possible U.S. withdrawal from the treaty.[3] VDoc implementation is less contested, but efforts to modernize the agreement to make it relevant to current security challenges have repeatedly failed.

The purpose of this report is not to rehash the history of the CAC regime's demise. CFE follow-on negotiations became entangled with other (seemingly intractable) political and political-military disputes between Russia and other states-parties. Modernization of VDoc has become linked to those negotiations, and thus is hostage to the ongoing deadlock. The disputes surrounding OST implementation have largely foreclosed any discussion of updating its provisions. As a result, observers on all sides are extremely pessimistic about the short-term prospects for reviving the CAC regime in its current form. The scholar Łukasz Kulesa has noted that the existing regimes are "so contested and compromised that they are no longer feasible bases for an effective new system."[4] Yet even if the political disputes surrounding the CAC regime were to be resolved, today there would be no strategic logic in reviving its central pillar, CFE or A/CFE. The rationale for the CFE treaty—addressing a destabilizing quantity of conventional arms on the European continent—is no longer relevant in 2020. Today, large numbers of CFE-limited equipment are clearly no longer the primary threat, and quantity is no longer commensurate with capabilities in light of military-technological developments since the original treaty

---

3 Michael R. Gordon and Vivian Salama, "Trump Moves Closer to Ending Another Post-Cold War Treaty," *Wall Street Journal*, October 27, 2019.

4 Łukasz Kulesa, "The Future of Conventional Arms Control in Europe," *Survival*, Vol. 60, No. 4, 2018, p. 80.

was negotiated. In short, there is no existing framework for producing a CAC agreement relevant to current security challenges. This report aims to help identify such a framework by asking first-order questions about the military drivers of potential conflict and using the answers to suggest a menu of possible CAC measures to address those drivers.

Research Questions

The key research questions considered in this report are:

- What are the primary conventional military drivers of instability, potential conflict, and escalation between Russia and NATO in the period up to 2025?
- What CAC measures might address those drivers in order to reduce the possibility of unintended conflict through misunderstanding or miscalculation?

Methodology and Structure of the Report

We focused exclusively on addressing potential conflict involving NATO member states and Russia (and its ally Belarus);[5] we did not seek to devise CAC solutions to the other major security challenges in Europe, such as the protracted conflicts in the South Caucasus or in Ukraine. This choice might seem unorthodox because the existing CAC agreements all include states other than NATO allies and Russia (and not all allies are party to the three agreements). However, narrowing the scope in such a way not only makes the analytical task more manageable but also reflects the reality that the dynamics driving a potential Russia-NATO conflict differ significantly from those relevant to, for example, instability between Armenia and Azerbaijan.

---

[5] Of Russia's allies in the Collective Security Treaty Organization, Belarus is the only one geographically relevant to a potential Russia-NATO conflict.

In this report, we use *CAC* to refer to a broad range of measures, including CSBMs and other risk-reduction measures. Some argue that only "hard" measures, such as reductions and numerical ceilings, should be considered arms control; all other measures, by this definition, are CSBMs. There is some logic in this distinction, but by using a broader definition of CAC, the report avoids artificially excluding measures that might be relevant.

To design CAC measures germane to current security challenges, we begin with an examination of the potential *military* drivers of conflict between Russia and NATO; specifically, those that such measures could plausibly address. We therefore deliberately excluded those drivers of conflict that a CAC regime could not address; specifically, potential political drivers of conflict, such as domestic instability, were beyond the scope of the study. Further, we excluded nonconventional military drivers of conflict, such as those related to nuclear weapons, cyber, and so-called *gray zone activities*, such as disinformation campaigns or economic coercion.[6] Deliberate acts of preplanned aggression were also beyond the scope. Although arms control can complicate war planning, it cannot stop a state from going to war if it is determined to do so. More broadly, we largely exclude discussion of states' intentions in this study, focusing instead on capabilities and related military dynamics.

To be clear, these drivers were excluded not because of a determination of their relevance (or irrelevance) to current NATO-Russia security dynamics, but rather because a CAC regime would have no bearing upon them. Therefore, the threat perceptions and conflict scenarios discussed in this report are not, by definition, a complete accounting of all possible roads to war. Instead, they focus on one important category of drivers: those found in the conventional military domain.

---

[6] The *gray zone* has been defined as "the operational space between peace and war, involving coercive actions to change the status quo below a threshold that, in most cases, would prompt a conventional military response, often by blurring the line between military and nonmilitary actions and the attribution for events" (Lyle J. Morris, Michael J. Mazarr, Jeffrey W. Hornung, Stephanie Pezard, Anika Binnendijk, and Marta Kepe, *Gaining Competitive Advantage in the Gray Zone: Response Options for Coercive Aggression Below the Threshold of Major War*, Santa Monica, Calif.: RAND Corporation, RR-2942-OSD, 2019, p. 7).

In addition to the conventional military drivers of conflict, we also sought to address the early stages of such a potential conflict. Specifically, we examined which elements of posture, force structure, capabilities, and doctrines contribute to escalation early in a potential conflict.

In short, the first stage of our research was devoted to attempting to identify, in as systematic a way as possible, the problem set that a CAC regime could plausibly address. We did so using two different sets of inputs. First, we ascertained perspectives on these issues from several of the key states involved, through analysis of published documents and interviews in NATO member-state capitals with government officials and nongovernmental experts. Additionally, we documented Russian views on the possible causes of conflict through a review of statements by Moscow's political and military leadership and relevant Russian military-scientific publications. These threat perceptions are discussed in Chapter Two. Second, we tasked RAND Corporation military experts with developing four conflict scenarios involving Russia and NATO, which are presented in vignette form in Chapter Three. The four scenarios address, respectively, potential roads to war in the maritime, ground, and air domains, and the initial stages of combat following war initiation. The threat perceptions research and scenarios were discussed at a workshop in Berlin in January 2019. The project team, the RAND specialists who built the scenarios, and experts from across the German government attended that meeting, the purposes of which were to distill insights about possible paths to conflict and to identify similarities and differences among the allied views, Russian perceptions, and the scenarios.

We begin our report with research on the causes of potential conflict because there is, in fact, no consensus among NATO allies—let alone between NATO and Russia—on what capabilities, deployments, postures, and other factors might be destabilizing. This divergence in perspectives contrasts with the intra-NATO discussion in the years leading up to the negotiations on the original CFE. At that time, as the scholar Richard Falkenrath wrote, "All members of the alliance agreed that an imbalance of conventional weaponry existed in Europe, and that the foremost objective of the CFE negotiations should be a substantial reduction in the most threatening [Warsaw Pact] forces in Central Europe."[7] NATO allies agreed that the imbalance favoring the Warsaw Pact—and the concentration of Pact forces in Central Europe—would make it possible for the latter to achieve a quick victory in a conventional conflict, forcing NATO to resort to nuclear use. Therefore the alliance's goal for the talks became "the elimination of the Warsaw Pact's ability to conduct short-warning, large-scale sustained offensive operations, without undermining NATO's ability to implement its strategy for forward defense."[8] Although some allies had additional concerns particular to their respective strategic circumstances (Norway, for example, worried about Soviet forces massing near their shared border), all essentially agreed that the alliance faced a specific security challenge that arms control could address. Today, above and beyond the well-known lack of consensus in threat perceptions at the strategic level (e.g., southern European allies' greater concern about threats from the south versus eastern allies' focus on threats from the east), there is also a divergence about which specific Russian capabilities, postures, and deployments pose security challenges that CAC could mitigate. Without an answer to that question, there is no logic to pursuing CAC negotiations.

The threat-perceptions research and scenario-building exercise provided a variety of data on the potential causes of conflict between Russia and NATO. We broke these data down into specific events on the road to war—in other words, specific escalatory actions that precipitate conflict. These events, in turn, were further disaggregated into what we termed *military factors*: generalizable categories for military dynamics that had an escalatory effect. Ultimately, we identified 14 such factors. (See the full list and discussion in Chapter Four.) Some events featured more than one factor. For example, an event in one scenario was a large Russian no-notice "snap" exercise in Belarus.[9]

---

[7] Richard Falkenrath, *Shaping Europe's Military Order: The Origins and Consequences of the CFE Treaty*, Cambridge, Mass.: MIT Press, 1995, p. 5.

[8] Falkenrath, 1995, pp. 11–12.

[9] *Snap exercises* refer to unscheduled drills with little or no warning provided to the troops involved in the training or to other states. Russia has conducted a number of such exercises

This event had an escalatory effect because it was (1) *a training exercise in a strategically sensitive location* and it involved (2) *massing of forces*. Because our search for possible conflict scenarios and threat perceptions was not intended to be exhaustive, we did not treat the frequency of the appearance of a given factor as a definitive indicator of its importance to potential conflict. However, certain patterns did emerge, and certain factors clearly are more relevant than others—these are documented in Chapter Four.

Up to this point, our research process was intentionally divorced from policy considerations regarding CAC, with the exception of the limitations regarding scope discussed previously. We sought to develop our understanding of the military drivers of conflict and escalation in Europe without reference to whether—and, if so, how—a CAC regime could mitigate those drivers. If we had brought in CAC policy considerations at an earlier stage, we would likely have limited the study to those factors most likely to be addressed by the existing CAC instruments, not necessarily those most relevant to potential NATO-Russia conflict.

Having developed a list of the key military drivers of possible escalation, we then sought to identify possible CAC measures to address them. We did so through our own original research on these measures and through a second workshop in Berlin in June 2019. To reinforce the purposeful separation between analysis of conflict drivers and proposals to address them, we invited a group of experts—specifically, those with expertise on CAC regimes—who were not at the first workshop to give presentations at this event. In advance of the workshop, we provided these experts with different sets of the identified drivers and asked them to develop potential CAC measures to address them. During the workshop—which, in addition to the invited specialists, was attended by the project team and German government experts—we discussed and further refined these proposals. Finally, we systematized those proposals, incorporating insights from original research and previous RAND studies on CAC, particularly a range of exten-

in recent years. There is a legitimate military purpose to snap exercises—to test readiness, primarily—but they tend to exacerbate threat perceptions of other states.

sive studies from the period of 1989–1999 sponsored by the Office of the Secretary of Defense. The results (Chapter Five) are presented as a menu of possible options for policymakers to consider in potential future negotiations. See Figure 1.1 for a summary of the methodology used in the report.

Literature Review

In the 1980s and early 1990s, CAC was widely studied and debated in the strategic community and among prominent academic scholars of international relations. Research at that time focused on the fundamental question of how a CAC regime could contribute to stability in Europe; in other words, what problems CAC could address, and how.[10] After the signing of A/CFE in 1999, not only did the overall number of publications on the subject decrease significantly, but the focus of those that did appear also shifted. Many, if not most, of the studies published before 2014 focused on options to address the political disputes that led to the effective collapse of CFE and the failure to ratify the adapted

Figure 1.1
Methodology

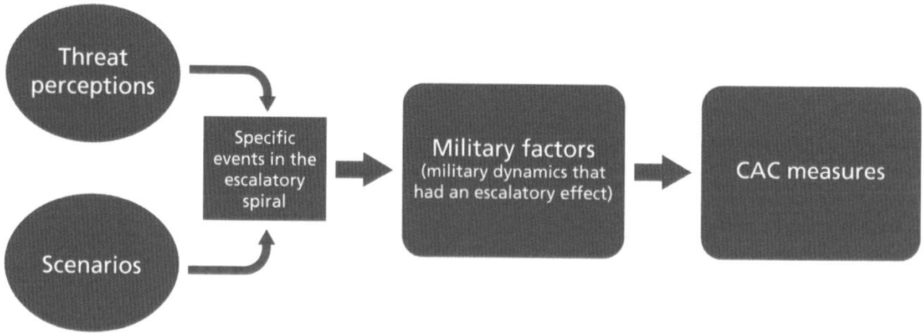

[10] See, for example, Paul K. Davis, *Toward a Conceptual Framework for Operational Arms Control in Europe's Central Region*, Santa Monica, Calif.: RAND Corporation, R-3704-USDP, 1988, and Barry R. Posen, "Crisis Stability and Conventional Arms Control," *Daedalus*, Vol. 120, No. 1, Winter 1991.

treaty.[11] The new concepts that were proposed in this period reflected the pre-2014 security environment, when tensions between Russia and NATO were considerably lower than they are today. For example, the arms control expert Hans-Joachim Schmidt proposed the concept of "verified transparency" on the assumption that a CAC regime need only provide for transparency and not limitations of any kind.[12] More broadly, before 2014, CAC had been reconceived as a means of creating a cooperative security environment in Europe, and specifically between NATO and Russia; rather than enhancing stability in relations between potential adversaries, it was hoped that arms control could accelerate the transformation of those relations toward genuine partnership. Capturing the spirit of the time, one scholar wrote, "To end mistrust and suspicion, NATO and Russia must re-engage in the concept of cooperative security. Conventional arms control is one possible way to do so."[13]

Following Moscow's annexation of Crimea and invasion of eastern Ukraine in 2014, tensions between NATO and Russia increased

---

11 Anne Witkowsky, Sherman Garnett, and Jeff McCaulsand, *Salvaging the Conventional Arms Forces in Europe Treaty Regime: Options for Washington*, Brookings Arms Control Series, No. 2, Washington, D.C.: Brookings Institution, March 23, 2010; Paul Schulte, "The Precarious State of Flux of the Conventional Armed Forces in Europe Treaty (CFE)," Carnegie Council for Ethics in International Affairs, June 2, 2011; Jeffrey D. McCausland, *The Future of the CFE Treaty: Why It Still Matters*, New York, N.Y.: EastWest Institute, June 2009; and Wolfgang Zellner, "Can This Treaty Be Saved? Breaking the Stalemate on Conventional Forces in Europe," *Arms Control Today*, Vol. 39, No. 7, September 2009. For Russian perspectives, see Andrei Zagorskii, "Krizis kontrolya obychnykh vooruzhennykh sil v Evrope—sud'ba Dogovora ob obychnykh vooruzhennykh silakh," in A. Orlov, ed., *Mezhdunarodnye organizatsii i obespechenie mezhdunarodnoi bezopasnosti, Tom 19*, Moscow: Rossiiskoi assotsiatsii mezhdunarodnykh issledovanii, 2009; and Anatolii Antonov and Rodion Ayumov, *Kontrol' nad obychnymi vooruzheniyami v Evrope—Konets rezhima ili istoriya s prodolzheniem?* Moscow: PIR-Center, 2012.

12 See Hans-Joachim Schmidt, *Verified Transparency: New Conceptual Ideas for Conventional Arms Control in Europe*, PRIF Report No. 119, Frankfurt am Main, Germany: Peace Research Institute Frankfurt, 2013. See also Jacek Durkalec, "Rethinking Conventional Arms Control in Europe: A Transparency-Centered Approach," *Strategic File*, No. 7 (34), Polish Institute of International Affairs, September 2013.

13 Ulrich Kühn, "Conventional Arms Control 2.0," *Journal of Slavic Military Studies*, Vol. 26, No. 2, 2013.

significantly. Because the pre-2014 vision of cooperative security was now widely considered a fantasy, CAC studies written since then have focused on how to address this more-adversarial dynamic. Several authors have pointed to the potential for CAC to mitigate tensions along the NATO-Russia frontier, specifically in the Baltic region.[14] These studies have usefully contributed to a discussion of what measures might be relevant to the current security environment. However, the measures they recommend are largely grounded in relatively vague understandings of the drivers of conflict, such as "uncertainty" and "show of force."[15] None takes the bottom-up, first principles–based approach used in this report. For example, one such study seeks to prevent a "destabilizing build-up of strength along the contact line between Russia and NATO," but does not define which kind of build-ups would qualify as destabilizing and why.[16] Corentin Brustlein's 2018 publication on strategic stability and arms control is a prominent exception.[17] He provided recommendations for arms control measures using an extensive analysis of current Russian and NATO capabilities and how they might undermine strategic stability in the regional European context. However, the scope of his study is both broader than that of this report in that it covers measures to "alleviate concerns regarding the survivability of second strike forces" and more narrow in

---

[14] See, for example, Wolfgang Richter, *Sub-Regional Arms Control for the Baltics: What is Desirable? What is Feasible?* Deep Cuts Working Paper, No. 8, July 2016.

[15] Wolfgang Zellner, Philip Remler, Wolfgang Richter, Andrei Zagorski, Evgeny P. Buzhinsky, Vladislav L. Chernov, Ali Serdar Erdurmaz, Marc Finaud, Cornelius Friesendorf, P. Terrence Hopmann, Łukasz Kulesa, Igors Rajevs, Benjamin Schaller, Hans-Joachim Schmidt, Niklas Schörning, Oleg Shakirov, and Simon Weiss, *Reducing the Risks of Conventional Deterrence in Europe: Arms Control in the NATO-Russia Contact Zones*, Vienna, Austria: Organization for Security and Co-operation in Europe (OSCE) Network of Think Tanks and Academic Institutions, December 2018, p. 13.

[16] Evgeny Buzhinskiy and Oleg Shakirov, *Outlines for Future Conventional Arms Control in Europe: A Sub-Regional Regime in the Baltics*, London, UK: European Leadership Network, September 2019, p. 2.

[17] Corentin Brustlein, *The Erosion of Strategic Stability and the Future of Arms Control in Europe*, Paris, France: Institut français des relations internationales, IFRI Proliferation Papers, No. 60, November 2018.

that it focuses on drivers of instability at the strategic level.[18] That said, on matters where the scope of the two does overlap, Brustlein reached similar conclusions to those presented in this report.

A number of other recent Western think tank reports have focused on the challenges associated with reviving the current regimes, with a broad consensus that overcoming them is impossible due to the divergent interests and approaches of key parties.[19] As one of these studies concluded, "the preconditions for initiating negotiations on arms control in the OSCE area are not in place at this particular point in time."[20] Russian studies on the subject tend to reach the same conclusion.[21] This pessimism is certainly warranted, but the deadlock among the governments should be seen as an opportunity for nongovernmental researchers to contribute new ideas and concepts that are ready for the moment when the deadlock breaks.

Caveats

In addition to the scope limitations noted above, a number of caveats should be mentioned regarding the findings of this study. First, this report is not intended to generate actionable proposals for implementation within existing negotiating formats, such as the OSCE-based discussions on VDoc modernization or any potential CFE follow-on

---

[18] Brustlein, 2018, p. 65.

[19] Hans-Joachim Schmidt, *A Fresh Start of Conventional Arms Control in Europe Will Face Many Structural Problems*, PRIF Report No. 151, Frankfurt am Main, Germany: Peace Research Institute Frankfurt, 2017; Peter van Ham, *Modernizing Conventional Arms Control in the Euro-Atlantic Region*, The Hague: Netherlands Institute of International Relations, September 2018.

[20] Johan Engvall, Gudrun Persson (ed.), Robert Dalsjö, Carolina Vendil Pallin, and Mike Winnerstig, *Conventional Arms Control: A Way Forward or Wishful Thinking?* Stockholm, Sweden: Swedish Defence Research Agency, FOI-R--4586--SE, April 2018, p. 69.

[21] See, for example, Oleg Shakirov, *Budushchee Venskogo dokumenta: perspektivy razvitiya mer ukrepleniya doveriya i bezopasnosti v Evrope*, Moscow: Trialog, 2019; and Yurii Belobrov, "Nadezhdy evropeitsev po vozrozhdeniyu deistvennogo KOVE eshche ne ugasli," *Mezhdunarodnaya zhizn'*, No. 6, 2017.

talks. We sought to develop CAC measures without the encumbrance of the traditional division between "soft" CSBMs in VDoc and "hard" arms control of CFE. Moreover, we also started from a blank slate instead of proposing changes or amendments to the current regimes. Our approach was to devise measures based on their relevance to mitigating the drivers of potential conflict—as opposed to their relationship to existing agreements. Although this method points to the most potentially effective measures, it does not provide policymakers with proposed solutions to the problems of the day, such as how best to modernize VDoc.

Second, and relatedly, we do not offer solutions to the political disputes surrounding the current CAC regimes. Both A/CFE entry-into-force and the CFE follow-on talks failed because of disputes over Russia's military presence on the sovereign territory of Georgia and Moldova without host-nation consent, a key CFE principle. (Since then, of course, Russia has annexed Crimea and invaded eastern Ukraine, creating more host-nation consent-related issues.) These are very real political impediments to progress on CAC. Our report does not provide recommendations to address them.

Third, this report offers suggestions for measures that might become part of a potential future CAC agreement, but it does not propose a diplomatic strategy to reach such an agreement. All multilateral security arrangements involving adversaries are extremely difficult to negotiate. CAC, given the political baggage mentioned previously, is even more challenging. There would need to be careful consideration of potential trade-offs that would be necessary to reach consensus; an agreement must be seen as beneficial by all parties. Additionally, decisions about what to do with the existing agreements in the context of a negotiation over a new one—whether to keep, discard, or amend those agreements—would be required. Those decisions would be complicated by the divergence in participants in the different regimes: There are 57 states that participate in VDoc, 30 states-parties to CFE, and 34 states-parties to OST. The measures that we discuss in this report are relevant only to NATO member states and Russia and potentially Belarus, although they could be embedded in a broader agreement involving more states. A decision about participants would, in turn, affect the venue for talks: the NATO-Russia Council in Brussels or the OSCE in Vienna.

Although these caveats do limit the immediate practical applicability of the findings of this study, avoiding these three issues allowed for a more intellectually rigorous, less politically constrained look at the core issues. The proposed measures and surrounding discussions presented here are designed to stimulate thought and inform future discussions on the development of CAC measures that can address the security challenges of the 21st century.

CHAPTER TWO

Threat Perceptions

This chapter presents research on the perceptions of a range of key states regarding the military drivers of potential conflict between Russia and NATO. The purpose here is to understand better what policymakers and the broader strategic communities in these countries believe might be the causes of potential escalation. Such an understanding should inform the requirements for any potential future CAC regime in Europe. The chapter begins with views from nine NATO allies, largely derived from interviews with experts in participating states' capitals. The second section presents Russian perspectives on the same issues through an analysis of leadership statements and writings of military strategists. Finally, we offer some observations based on these two lines of research. See Figure 2.1 for a map showing the locations referenced in this chapter.

Views of Select NATO Allies

This section provides an overview of the threat perceptions of select NATO allies regarding potential conflict with Russia. The analysis is based on interviews conducted by the project team between November 2018 and March 2019 in the following countries: Estonia, Germany, Latvia, Lithuania, Norway, Poland, Romania, the United Kingdom, and the United States. We have supplemented these findings with relevant national policy documents and assessments where appropriate.

In total, the project team conducted 38 interviews with 56 experts, including 40 government officials and 16 nongovernmental

Figure 2.1
Map of the NATO-Russia Frontier

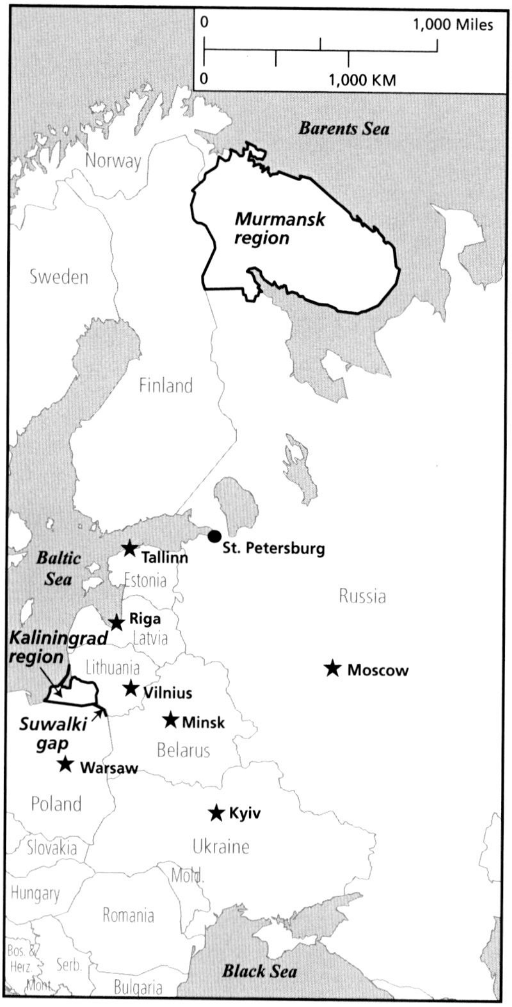

experts from academic and research institutions. All interviewees spoke in a personal capacity on a not-for-attribution basis; their views should not be considered statements of official policy.

The interviews sought to examine issues that could spark conflict between NATO and Russia. We purposefully did not focus on potential political drivers of conflict and instead aimed to better understand allies' concerns regarding a potential surprise attack and their views on which Russian capabilities (or combination of capabilities) would enable such an attack. We also asked about the potential drivers of unintended escalation between NATO and Russia, focusing particularly on conflict driven by misinterpretation of military factors rather than deliberate, politically driven escalation. The definition of "unintended" was intentionally left open to stimulate more-engaging discussions and help the project team better understand the full range of possible pathways to conflict. We grouped our findings into four main categories: potential threats posed by Russian capabilities, perceptions regarding NATO and Russian vulnerabilities, sources of escalation risk, and perceptions regarding Russian intentions.

Threat Perceptions Regarding Russian Capabilities

During the Cold War, NATO member states generally shared common threat perceptions. Today, there is a debate over the nature and extent of the potential Russian threat both at the strategic level and at the tactical level, where allies also have differing views about which Russian capabilities are particularly threatening. There were, however, some points of consensus from the interviews. These included:

- Current Russian capabilities and posture are not so threatening in themselves that they could start an escalatory spiral. However, interlocutors believed that, by 2025, Russian capabilities could improve enough to create insecurities and thus potentially spark a conflict.
- In most cases, it is the combination of different Russian capabilities rather than one single capability that caused the most concern.
- Russian capabilities could be used to delay or prevent NATO access and deployment to certain areas, a phenomenon referred to as anti-access/area denial (A2/AD) by interviewees.[1]

---

[1] As Michael Kofman notes, A2/AD is not a Russian operational concept (Michael Kofman, "It's Time to Talk About A2/AD: Rethinking the Russian Military Challenge," *War on the*

Interviewees identified the following factors as being of particular concern: Russian strike capabilities, Russian structural advantages in the land domain (mass, positioning, and readiness), snap exercises, and so-called A2/AD capabilities. There was near-consensus regarding the threats associated with Russian strike capabilities and massing ability; the other factors were highlighted by some interlocutors but not others.

Our interlocutors assessed that Russia's extensive strike capabilities from multiple platforms (ground, sea, and air) covering short, medium, and long ranges could be used to prevent NATO forces from deploying (e.g., by targeting strategic transport infrastructure or air bases in NATO countries) or to support Russian ground operations, as was the case in Syria. Russia could also employ them (particularly land-based missiles) against NATO targets with little or no warning. In Europe, the short flight times to key NATO targets for a number of Russian precision-guided munition (PGM) systems allows Moscow to hold critical combat nodes permanently at risk. Interviewees mentioned the following systems: the 3M-14 *Kalibr*, a sea-launched cruise missile (SLCM) with an estimated range of 1,500–2,500 km; the *Iskander*, a road-mobile, ballistic missile system with an estimated range of 400–500 km; and the 9M729, an intermediate-range ground-launched cruise missile that NATO allies assessed had been deployed at the time our interviews took place. In terms of future threats, interviewees highlighted the new *Kalibr-M* (4,500-km range), expected in late 2020.[2]

Interviewees believed that Russia has structural advantages in the land domain because of three key factors: *mass* (i.e., a large number of tanks, artillery systems, and troops), *positioning* (a high concentration of capabilities relatively near borders with NATO), and *readiness* (both the high general readiness of forces and the ability for rapid mobilization and maneuver to support rapid deployment in a crisis or in the context of a surprise attack). Our interlocutors noted that these advantages could be multiplied with additional forward-deployed enablers for rapid maneuver, particularly in Belarus. Such deployments would

---

Rocks, September 5, 2019).

2 "Istochnik: v Rossii razrabatyvayut novuyu krylatuyu raketu 'Kalibr-M'," TASS, January 19, 2019.

further reduce warning time. Official policy documents support this assessment. For instance, Lithuania's 2019 National Threat Assessment argued that, in the early stage of a conflict, "Russia's ability to rapidly generate forces" would enable "it to gain . . . an obvious military advantage over the neighboring states."[3]

Some respondents stressed that this structural advantage could be further exploited via snap exercises, which can provide cover for an attack. A 2019 NATO Parliamentary Assembly report echoes this argument: "Snap exercises can test force readiness, but they are also a means of testing adversary reaction, as they may confuse an observer about Russia's real capabilities and intentions." Russia, the report contends, has used such exercises to "mask . . . aggression."[4]

Respondents identified the deployment of what they called A2/AD layered protection as a concern. They assessed that the number, capability, and mobility of so-called A2/AD systems (both anti-air and anti-ship) provide Russia with an advantage in the Baltic region and in the Black Sea, where more-capable over-the-horizon radar systems have been deployed. Specific systems mentioned during the interviews include the S-300 and S-400 (mobile anti-air systems); K-300P *Bastion-P* (anti-ship, mobile coastal defense system, a variant of P-800 *Oniks* supersonic anti-ship cruise missile); and electronic warfare (EW) systems (e.g., mobile *Krasukha*-4 systems) for such activities as radar signals jamming and Global Positioning System spoofing. Many also argued that Russia benefited from a space-time advantage; NATO forces would be highly vulnerable if they were to enter the Baltic region or the Black Sea once hostilities had started.

To put the capability-focused threat perception in geographic context, Figure 2.2 provides a visual representation of the ranges of Russian strike and air defense capabilities.

---

[3] Ministry of National Defence, *National Threat Assessment 2019*, Vilnius, Lithuania: State Security Department of the Republic of Lithuania, February 5, 2019, p. 21.

[4] Lara Martinho, *NATO Exercises—Evolution and Lessons Learned*, Brussels, Belgium: Sub-Committee on Future Security and Defence Capabilities, Defence and Security Committee, NATO Parliamentary Assembly, October 13, 2019, p. 4.

Figure 2.2
Russian Strike and Air Defense Ranges in Europe

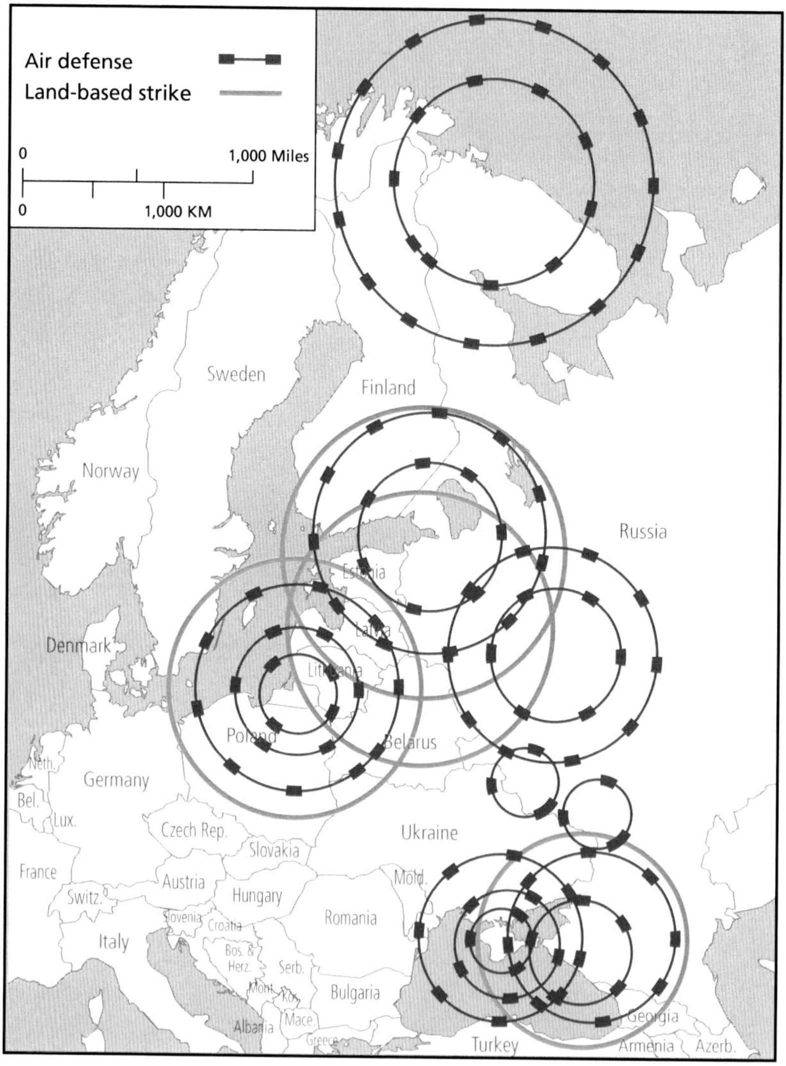

SOURCE: Ian Williams, "The Russia – NATO A2AD Environment," Missile Threat, Center for Strategic and International Studies, January 3, 2017. Recreated with permission of the CSIS Missile Defense Project.

Vulnerability Perceptions

Our interlocutors identified two key locations that represent vulnerabilities for both NATO and Russia: the regions of Kaliningrad and Murmansk.[5] The former is both a Russian vulnerability and a potential threat to NATO because of its position between Poland and Lithuania on the Baltic Sea. Lithuania's 2019 National Threat Assessment highlights that Russian military activity in Kaliningrad "negatively affects Lithuania's security environment and increases the risk of unintentional incidents."[6] The Murmansk region, which is on the Norwegian border, hosts Russia's Northern Fleet and command posts, administrative support, and operational capabilities at air and naval bases. As the Norwegian Intelligence Service's *Focus 2019* report states, the Murmansk region constitutes a "military center of gravity" for Russia, with the surrounding Barents Sea acting as "the key deployment area for the Northern Fleet and its strategic submarines."[7] The proximity to the border makes the area strategically vulnerable to NATO, while the host of capabilities stationed there pose a threat to NATO.

In terms of geography, interviewees argued that southeastern Europe is far less likely to be the locus of a potential Russia-NATO clash than northeastern Europe. There is no land border between a NATO member state and Russia there. NATO has more strategic depth in the southeast than in the northeast, and geographical peculiarities that create vulnerabilities, such as Kaliningrad and Murmansk, are absent. That said, NATO is at a significant disadvantage, capabilities-wise, in the Black Sea region vis-à-vis Russia. RAND scholars Stephen Flanagan and Irina Chindea have noted that whereas Russia has deployed advanced coastal, air-defense, early-warning, and EW systems in addition to its air and naval power-projection forces, "NATO's tailored forward presence" in the Black Sea region "is quite limited, and the more capable European governments seem uninterested in contribut-

---

5 *Kaliningrad* and *Murmansk* are used here to refer to the regions, not the eponymous regional capitals.

6 Ministry of National Defence, 2019, p. 22.

7 Norwegian Intelligence Service, *Focus 2019*, Oslo, Norway, February 11, 2019, p. 25.

ing troops to the multinational brigade in Romania or augmenting the NATO maritime presence [there]."[8]

From a capability perspective, interviewees identified vulnerabilities that could both reduce Russian incentives to go to war with NATO but paradoxically increase the incentives to escalate such a war quickly if it were to occur. Respondents assessed that although the balance of forces in the Baltic region might be skewed in Russia's favor at the beginning of a potential conflict, the Russian military does not have the capacity to sustain or regenerate forces in the face of severe casualties or loss of equipment. This inability to sustain a prolonged war might cause Russian commanders to escalate early in a conflict in order to end it quickly.

Sources of Escalation Risk

In addition to threats and vulnerabilities, the interviews explored the risk of unintended escalation. The following six escalatory factors were identified.

1. Proximity breeds instability. During a crisis, NATO and Russian forces would be almost immediately in close proximity, and thus both would be extremely vulnerable. Proximity and the awareness of this vulnerability would increase tension and, in turn, raise the chances of misperception or miscalculation. Although it might not be enough to justify a first strike or initiate a conflict, proximity is potentially a key driver of rapid escalation should a conflict be triggered elsewhere.

2. A window of perceived unilateral vulnerability creates first-strike incentives. A military build-up or arms race could progress to a point at which one of the two sides feels threatened beyond an acceptable threshold and decides to strike first to preempt the other side from achieving a decisive advantage. The perception of being exposed to unacceptable risk because of the other side's newly acquired and deployed capabilities could lead one side to decide to make the first move.

---

[8] Stephen J. Flanagan, and Irina A. Chindea, *Russia, NATO, and Black Sea Security Strategy: Regional Perspectives from a 2019 Workshop* , Santa Monica, Calif.: RAND Corporation, CF-405-OSD, 2019, p. 12.

3. Geography creates escalatory pressure. Geographical vulnerabilities could drive escalation. The concentration of Russian military assets in the Murmansk region on the border with Norway is a major vulnerability for Moscow, although that border itself is only lightly defended from the Norwegian side and thus a vulnerability for NATO. A similar dynamic is in play with Kaliningrad. Neither situation in itself is likely to trigger a conflict, but both could provide an incentive for rapid horizontal escalation in these vulnerable spots should a conflict begin elsewhere.

4. Snap exercises can be (or can be interpreted as) a cover for a surprise attack. The increased number of Russian no-notice snap exercises creates uncertainty about Moscow's intentions and heightens threat perceptions. Several interlocutors argued that through the snap exercises Russia is attempting to establish a new normal characterized by a high level of unpredictability in order to enhance its leverage.

5. Ambiguity itself can be a source of escalatory pressure. Interviewees believed ambiguity about Russia's intentions was itself a potential source of escalation.

6. Concerns about NATO unity create escalatory pressure. Some NATO allies are concerned that others in the alliance have an incentive to escalate a conflict with Russia rapidly in its early stages to remove any doubts about Russian actions and ensure a NATO response. Estonia's National Security Concept notes that "In the event of an attack, Estonia will defend its entire territory from the state border onwards and will continue military resistance even in areas over which it may have temporarily lost control." To ensure the credibility of deterrence, "NATO must be capable of immediate collective counteraction everywhere on the Alliance's territory."[9] In other words, Estonia will respond immediately to any perceived Russian attack in order to trigger an alliance response. The fear that other NATO allies will downplay Russian actions to avoid a war could incentivize early escalation.

---

[9] Ministry of Defence of the Republic of Estonia, *National Security Concept 2017*, Tallinn, Estonia, 2017, pp. 11–12.

Perceptions Regarding Russian Intentions

A number of interviewees expressed skepticism that the Russian military could ever inadvertently escalate a conflict; its actions would always be intentional. Four related reasons were offered. First, some made the case that NATO's activities could never be misperceived as genuinely threatening to Russia; therefore, any Russian escalatory action *by definition* would be a sign of deliberate, intentional aggression. Second, others made the case that the Kremlin is calculating and opportunistic, and therefore any Russian military action would be the result of a deliberate political decision, not a miscalculation. Third, some argued that the Russian political-military leadership exercises tight control over decisionmaking, and therefore no tactical-level situation would be allowed to escalate without authorization from the top. Finally, interviewees portrayed Russia as a strategic actor, in the sense that it would not allow a situation to escalate unless it perceived that gains would be higher than costs. The Turkish shootdown of a Russian jet in Syria in 2015 was cited as a case in point: Moscow deliberately behaved provocatively toward Ankara, and equally deliberately sought to deescalate the crisis once Turkey retaliated. The takeaway was that Moscow can avoid an escalation spiral if the political will exists to do so.

These expressed views are consistent with the sorts of cognitive biases that Robert Jervis highlighted in his classic work on misperception:

> [S]tates are more likely to overestimate the hostility of others than to underestimate it. States are prone to exaggerate the reasonableness of their own positions and the hostile intent of others; indeed, the former process feeds the latter. Statesmen, wanting to think well of themselves and their decisions, often fail to appreciate others' perspectives, and so greatly underestimate the extent to which their [own] actions can be seen as threats.
>
> When their intentions are peaceful, statesmen think that others will understand their motives and therefore will not be threatened by the measures they are taking in their own self-defense.[10]

[10] Robert Jervis, "War and Misperception," *Journal of Interdisciplinary History*, Vol. 18, No. 4, Spring 1988, pp. 688–689.

Elsewhere, Jervis writes that a country's lack of recognition that its "own actions could be seen as menacing and the concomitant belief that the other's hostility can only be explained by its aggressiveness help explain how conflicts can easily expand beyond that which an analysis of the objective situation would indicate is necessary."[11] In other words, the views voiced by interviewees about Russia are, in themselves, a potential escalatory factor. Effective arms control could help address them by reassuring parties about the other side's lack of aggressive intentions, but they also pose a challenge to pursuing arms control, which rests on an assumption that *both* sides would prefer to avoid conflict.

Russian Threat Perceptions

This section explores Russian threat perceptions regarding NATO's way of war and conventional military capabilities and posture. (It is important to note that Moscow does not differentiate between forces operating under NATO command and NATO member states' forces operating under national authority. Therefore, *NATO* in this section refers to both.) The research is derived from recent Russian civilian and military leadership speeches and articles, official government strategy documents, and writings of influential analysts in Russian military and defense policy journals. It should be noted that Moscow likely uses public critique of NATO's military capabilities to influence, intimidate, or divide allies, so careful analysis is required to separate genuine perceptions from propaganda. We have endeavored to highlight Russian threat perceptions that we judge to be sincerely held beliefs, based on the consistency with which they are raised over time and the number of different Russian officials and analysts who voice them. Evidence that the Russian military has made force-posture, capability-development, or other resource-related decisions that are consistent with stated threat

---

[11] Robert Jervis, *Perception and Misperception in International Politics*, Princeton, N.J.: Princeton University Press, 1976, p. 74.

perceptions is particularly dispositive. However, this analysis, by definition, involves a degree of subjective judgment.

Overview of Russian Threat Perceptions

Russian threat perceptions are driven by what many in Moscow see as an emerging hostile NATO strategy of neocontainment.[12] There is a consensus in the strategic community there that NATO poses a clear threat to Russia. NATO is seen as incrementally enhancing its capabilities to threaten Russia via force-posture enhancements, engaging in a creeping militarization of areas near Russia's borders, improving combat readiness through training, raising defense spending (when NATO already outspends Russia many times over), and undermining strategic and regional stability with new weapons or capabilities, such as ballistic missile defense (BMD) and long-range strike (LRS) platforms.

Russian leaders' threat perceptions regarding NATO reveal their own insecurities about their country's vulnerability to the alliance's combined military potential, particularly in the context of a hypothetical large-scale or protracted war. Russian strategists admit that their country is unlikely to be the stronger party in such a conflict, based on their calculations of the correlation of forces and their assessment that Russia will be unable to parry a massive NATO aerospace attack and manage command and control (C2) problems at scale.[13]

Among the specific conventional military challenges posed by NATO, Moscow considers the following factors to be the most threatening:

---

[12] In one example of many such statements, Valery Gerasimov, the Chief of the General Staff, stated in 2018 that NATO is taking "comprehensive, coordinated measures to contain Russia and discredit its role in international affairs" (Ministry of Defense of the Russian Federation, "Chief of General Staff General of the Army Valery Gerasimov Holds Briefing for Foreign Military Attaches," webpage, December 5, 2018).

[13] See, for example, I. A. Fedotov, "Tendentsii razvitiya operativno-strategicheskogo komandovaniya voennogo okruga na sovremennom etape formirovaniya Vooruzhennykh Sil Rossiiskoi Federatsii," *Vestnik AVN*, No. 4, 2016; and Konstantin Sivkov, "Nebesnye bastiony," *Voenno-promyshlennyi kur'er*, February 18, 2019.

- proximity and expansion of NATO military forces and related infrastructure near the borders of Russia
- particular geographic vulnerabilities, such as Kaliningrad and the high north
- long-range precision-strike capabilities that could be used against the Russian homeland and components of the nuclear triad
- NATO's advantage in the air domain.

We describe these Russian views in greater detail in the next section.

Russian Views of Threats in the Ground Domain

Russia's military doctrine lists the "deployment (buildup) of military forces of foreign states (or groups of states) on territories contiguous with the Russian Federation and its allies, and in adjacent seas, including for political and military pressure on the Russian Federation" as a top "external military danger."[14] It should come as no surprise, therefore, that Russian leaders have decried recent NATO deployments in the Baltic region.[15] That said, NATO forward deployments undertaken since 2014 in themselves are not seen as a threat to the military balance in the Baltic region, which is favorable to Russia.[16] Russian strategists consider the strongest operational contributions of land power to be during the opening phases of war (rapid response or deployment) and

---

[14] Ministry of Defense of the Russian Federation, *Military Doctrine of the Russian Federation*, Moscow, 2014.

[15] Defense Minister Sergei Shoygu recounted his understanding of NATO force posture enhancement near Russia: "since 2012, the numbers of NATO military contingents deployed on Russia's western borders have increased three-fold. Four battalion task forces and a US Army armored brigade are stationed in the Baltics and Poland; the multinational NATO divisions are headquartered in Poland and Romania. NATO priority forces have increased from 10,000 to 40,000, and their notice period has been reduced from 45 to 30 days" (President of Russia, "Expanded Meeting of the Defense Ministry Board," webpage, December 22, 2017).

[16] See Scott Boston, Michael Johnson, Nathan Beauchamp-Mustafaga, and Yvonne K. Crane, *Assessing the Conventional Force Imbalance in Europe: Implications for Countering Russian Local Superiority*, Santa Monica, Calif.: RAND Corporation, RR-2402, 2018.

in late phases of conflict (holding territory or consolidating gains).[17] The NATO Enhanced Forward Presence (eFP) battalions in Estonia, Latvia, Lithuania, and Poland in themselves are manifestly incapable of doing either. As one Russian parliamentarian put it, the four NATO eFP battalions are less troubling than the potential they create to receive additional or supporting forces in the future (or in a crisis):

> These four [eFP] battalions don't mean anything to us . . . however, the infrastructure involving a former airfield network, radar stations, and other military facilities . . . will allow for conducting various types of military activities.[18]

In other words, NATO's initiatives to bolster forward-deployed land forces have not been seen as a threat in themselves; it is the way in which they open the door for more-robust future deployments that concerns Moscow. If NATO were to deploy enough land forces to upset the military balance in the region—such as an additional large mechanized force (multi-brigade or multi-division)—on Russian borders, particularly if supported by theater-wide logistics, it would likely trigger a much stronger response. However, no such plans have been announced as of this writing.

Infrastructure

Russia also is concerned about NATO infrastructure; specifically, upgrades that improve U.S. power projection into Europe and facilitate NATO force flow to the east. This concern relates first and foremost to new infrastructure built near Russia: The military doctrine explicitly names the expansion of NATO member states' military infrastructure in close proximity to Russian borders as a top "external military danger."[19] Further from its borders, Russian planners likely observe

---

[17] S. V. Kuralenko, "Tendentsii izmeneniya kharaktera vooruzhennoi bor'by v voennykh konfliktakh pervoi poloviny XXI veka," *Voennaya mysl'*, No. 11, 2012.

[18] "Russia Has Resources to Respond to Deployment of New NATO Battalions in Baltics, Poland—Federation Council Member," Interfax, June 15, 2016.

[19] Ministry of Defense, 2014. The threat posed by NATO military infrastructure close to Russian borders is also mentioned in Russia's 2015 National Security Strategy (President of

with concern the establishment of command elements (such as the U.S. 2nd Fleet, NATO Atlantic Command, and Joint Enabling and Support Command), the improvement of main and alternate NATO transportation routes, the signing of cross-border transit agreements, and the creation of forward weapon and equipment-storage locations (such as U.S. Army Prepositioned Stocks [APS] and so-called European Activity Sets). Because Moscow views NATO combat potential holistically, Russian reactions to seemingly minor infrastructure improvements in Europe can seem disproportionate. For example, President Vladimir Putin noted in 2018, "Let's call things by their name, concerning Europe, the infrastructure being created there is offensive infrastructure."[20]

Modifications designed to improve reception and onward movement in Europe (for example, hardening of military ports and large NATO airfields, designating main deployment routes and improving bridges or roads along those routes, and expanding logistical hubs to support eastward movement towards the Russian and Belarusian borders) are of particular concern.[21] Improving or establishing new regional NATO C2 or coordination centers in eastern or northeastern Europe could be seen by Russian military planners as necessary preparations for wartime C2, as would NATO exercises that focus on long-distance power projection to the European continent or within it.

Geographic Sensitivities

Geographically, Kaliningrad is clearly the source of significant vulnerabilities. Russian planners are likely to react negatively to additional NATO long-range artillery or area-effects munitions that can range Kaliningrad, since such assets can target sensitive facilities, air-defense systems, the Baltic Fleet, and other Russian forces there with little warning. More broadly, despite what might seem on the map to be a significant strategic-depth advantage for Russia in the Baltic region,

---

Russia, On the Russian Federation's National Security Strategy, Presidential Edict No. 683, Moscow, December 31, 2015).

20 "Putin Slams 'Aggressive' New US Defence Strategy," *France 24*, December 22, 2017.

21 See President of Russia, "Board Meeting of the Ministry of Defense," December 18, 2018.

that frontier with NATO is actually extremely close to Russia's two largest cities, Moscow and St. Petersburg. In other words, the concentration of population centers near Western borders deprives Russia of an advantage from having a deeper interior. Unsurprisingly, Russia issued very harsh statements following announcements that Estonia's Amari military airfield would be modernized, claiming that advanced NATO fighters would be able to reach St. Petersburg in less than ten minutes if launched from the facility.[22] Russia is also concerned about defending its economic and military interests in the Arctic, and thus is extremely sensitive to potential NATO incursions from the north and surface and submarine deployments near its nuclear-powered ballistic missile submarine (SSBN) fleet bastions near Murmansk.

Long-Range Strike

NATO, and particularly U.S., (air, land, and sea-based) LRS capabilities are seen in Moscow as perhaps the single most threatening capability in the European regional context. To understand why, it is first necessary to explore Russia's underlying assumptions about NATO's way of war. Russian military strategists often state their belief that the center of gravity of modern warfare has shifted to the aerospace domain, a conclusion reached after observing U.S. and NATO military operations over the past twenty years. According to this view, modern conflicts will feature long-range precision strike weapons with greater lethality and ranges, launched en masse against enemy military forces and critical infrastructure.[23]

Russian scenarios for conflict with NATO focus heavily on the *initial period of war* (IPW), a short but intense period of adversary attack that can last from a few days to six weeks and is dominated by long-range precision strikes, air assaults from carrier aviation or other air forces, EW, counterspace strikes, and cyberattacks on critically

---

[22] "Russian Foreign Minister Calls Provocation Plans to Expand Estonia Amari Airfield for NATO Needs," Interfax, October 20, 2015.

[23] V. Gerasimov, "Generalnii shtab i oborona strany," *Voenno-promyshlennyi kur'er*, February 3, 2014.

important targets.[24] The IPW is viewed as decisive in Russian military strategy and is designed to "gain air superiority, degrade the enemy's nuclear strike potential, and create favorable conditions for ground forces operations."[25]

According to two Russian analysts, the "most rational" option for NATO military operations against Russia would be a surprise missile and air strike from stand-off ranges that targets Russian nuclear forces and other critical infrastructure. This strike would be enabled by multidomain intelligence, surveillance, and reconnaissance and information warfare.[26] Other analysts project initial strike packages involving 70 to 80 percent of NATO's available combat aviation, 30 percent of its naval aviation, and 60 percent of its Tomahawk cruise missile inventory during the IPW.[27]

Russian planners appear to have concluded that fending off even just a massed salvo of Tomahawk cruise missiles would likely overwhelm Russia's integrated air defenses (IADS).[28] Many key Russian critical infrastructure locations and military facilities remain partially or wholly without defenses capable of countering such an attack.[29] As demonstrated in Figure 2.3, strikes from notional launch points for the JASSM-ER air-launched cruise missile and the Tomahawk SLCM

---

[24] See S. G. Chekinov and S. A. Bogdanov, "Nachalnyye periody voin i ikh vliyanie na podgotovku strany k voine budushchego," *Voennaya mysl'*, No. 11, 2012; V. I. Vyspasnyak, A. M. Guralnik, and O. V. Tikhanychev, "Modelirovanie voennykh deistvii: istoriya, sovremennoe sostoyanie i perspektivy razvitiya," *Voennaya mysl'*, No. 7, 2014; and V. I. Litvinenko and I. P. Rusanov, "Osnovnye tendentsii ognevogo porazheniya v sovremennykh operatsiyakh (boevykh deistviyakh)," *Voennaya mysl'*, No. 10, 2014.

[25] Litvinenko and Rusanov, 2014.

[26] V. I. Polegaev and V. V. Alferov, "O neyadernom sderzhivanii, ego roli i meste v sisteme strategicheskogo sderzhivaniya," *Voennaya mysl'*, No. 7, 2015.

[27] Litvinenko and Rusanov, 2014.

[28] See A. M. Goncharov, "Voina budet vestis vo vsekh sredakh," *Vozdushno-Kosmicheskaya Oborona*, No. 6, 2015; and S. V. Yagolnikov, "Organizatsiya vozdushno-kosmicheskoi oborony v sovremennykh usloviyakh," *Vestnik AVN*, No. 2, 2016.

[29] O. Yu. Aksenov, Yu. N. Tretyakov, and Ye. N. Filin, "Osnovnye printspipy sozdaniya sistemy otsenki tekushego i prognoznogo usherba vazhneishim ob'ektam sistemy strategicheskogo sderznivaniya," *Voennaya mysl'*, No. 6, 2015.

Figure 2.3
Tomahawk and JASSM-ER Ranges from Hypothetical Launch Points

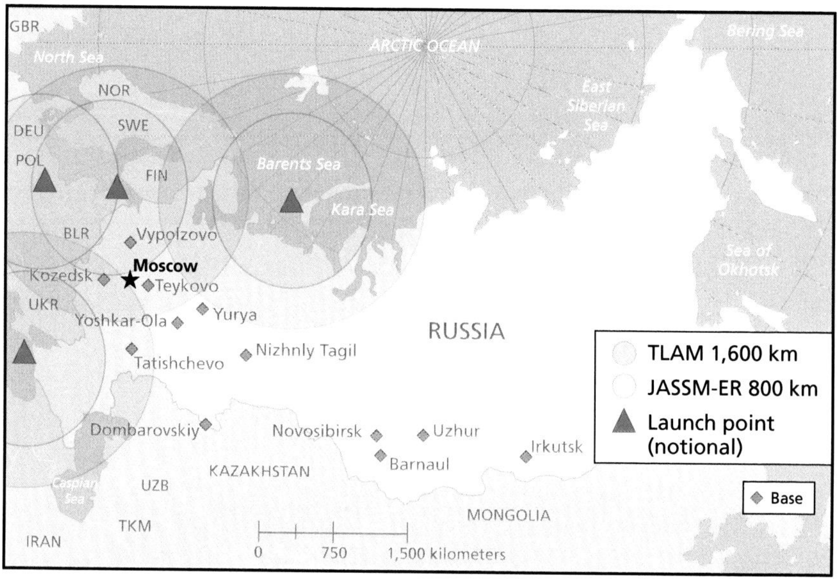

SOURCE: Defense Intelligence Agency, *Russia Military Power: Building a Military to Support Great Power Aspirations*, Washington: D.C, 2017; MissileThreat, "JASSM / JASSM ER (AGM-158A/B)," webpage, Center for Strategic and International Studies Missile Defense Project, last updated June 15, 2018; MissileThreat, "Tomahawk," webpage, Center for Strategic and International Studies Missile Defense Project, last updated November 4, 2019.
NOTE: The purple diamonds represent Russian Strategic Rocket Forces missile divisions. Ranges are the upper limits of published numbers, as provided by the CSIS Missile Threat project. The rings are approximations. The notional launch points are selected to highlight Russian concerns over NATO PGM range into Russia. It must be noted that PGM launch from these points would be very unlikely as platforms would be vulnerable to Russian IADS, coastal defenses, or naval defenses.

would cover a range of critical targets and population centers. It should be noted that the JASSM-XR, which has a 1,852-km range (over double the range of the JASSM-ER) is scheduled to come online in 2023.[30]

Given Russian views about the NATO way of war—specifically, that the IPW will be decisive and that the conflict will be aerospace-

[30] Kyle Mizokami, "America's Next Cruise Missile Will Strike from 1,000 Miles Away," *Popular Mechanics*, September 12, 2018.

dominant—and the challenges of defending against a cruise missile barrage given geography and NATO capabilities, Russian commanders likely anticipate having incentives to escalate rapidly in the opening phases of combat. Russia could seek to reduce NATO aerospace advantages by either conducting preemptive strikes against NATO LRS assets or high-intensity salvos in the opening hours or days of a conflict to achieve escalation dominance before NATO can take advantage of Russia's vulnerabilities.

For these reasons, Russia is likely to be extremely sensitive to the permanent or rotational presence of assets in Europe that are capable of launching long-range PGMs into Russia. These would include:

- aircraft carriers and associated carrier strike groups
- NATO surface combatant ships and submarines capable of firing long-range precision strikes or BMD interceptors (for example, Ticonderoga-class and Arleigh Burke–class destroyers in the U.S. Navy and similar combatants in other NATO navies)
- NATO combat aviation equipped with long-range missiles that can out-range Russian surface-to-air missiles or strike deep into sparsely defended areas
- highly capable fourth-plus and fifth-generation aircraft, particularly stealthy or low-observable platforms and munitions
- platforms with both conventional and nuclear-strike capabilities (strategic bombers, SSBNs with mixed payloads, or land-based cruise missile or missile interceptor launchers).

Naval Power as LRS Platform

Russia's primary concern about NATO naval power is its role in a potential massed aerospace attack, as discussed previously. Military analysts have deemed naval aviation and aircraft carriers as priority targets to neutralize early in a war because of their operational ranges. Moscow has also displayed sensitivity to certain classes of NATO ships (mostly those that carry long-range PGMs or are BMD-capable, like Arleigh Burke–class guided missile destroyers) in the Baltic and Black

Seas, often aggressively shadowing or "buzzing" these assets.[31] According to two prominent military analysts, the PGMs launched from these ships have a range encompassing most of western Russia, including major population and industrial centers, and such key military installations as strategic or tactical aviation bases.[32]

Ballistic Missile Defense Ambiguity

The Russian leadership frequently notes that BMD, particularly the U.S. BMD system, poses a threat to strategic stability.[33] Although strategic stability concerns are beyond the scope of this report, BMD has become entangled with LRS for Russia, and thus Russian officials claim it to be destabilizing to regional security dynamics in Europe. Certain classes of U.S. and allied naval ships equipped with the MK-41 launcher and Aegis system are capable of launching both ballistic missile interceptors and Tomahawk SLCMs, and they regularly operate in sensitive areas for Russia, such as the Baltic and Black Seas. When these ships are present in the Black or Baltic Seas, they pose threats to Russia both because of their SLCM capability and their BMD capability.

A modified version of the MK-41 is a component of the Aegis Ashore platform, which is used in the land-based elements of the European Phased Adaptive Approach BMD system in Romania and Poland. Thus, ground-based BMD has also become entangled with LRS for Russia. Russian officials have repeatedly stated that the land-based MK-41 launchers could be used to launch Tomahawks into Russia. As President Putin said, "to replace one missile with another presents no difficulty; you only need to replace the software, and no one will notice this."[34] Russian leaders believe these capabilities could be used with

---

[31] "Russian Flyby of USS Donald Cook in Baltic Sea Alarms Experts," *NBC News*, April 14, 2016.

[32] Sergei Vasil'ev and Vladimir Krivoruchko, "Nash nevnyatnyi otvet agressoru," *Voenno-promyshlennyi kur'er*, May 15, 2017.

[33] See, for example, President of Russia, 2015.

[34] "Bridge from Hellas. Vladimir Putin Visits Athens and the Holy Mountain of Athos," *Rossiiskaya Gazeta*, May 30, 2016.

little warning against Russian leadership positions, C2 nodes, nuclear forces, or other critical targets.

Additional Concerns Regarding NATO Airpower

In addition to air assets' roles as LRS platforms, Russia's concerns regarding NATO airpower are twofold: the challenge of monitoring NATO combat aviation forward-deployed to Europe, and an unfavorable correlation of forces. Although Russian officials often decry deployments of advanced airframes to Europe, military analysts point out that the current number of advanced aircraft on the continent is not destabilizing, but it is nonetheless an indication that future, more-problematic deployments are likely.[35] Both the proximity of these assets to Russian borders and their speed could pose a significant warning and monitoring burden on Moscow's early warning systems and could leave local commanders with an extremely short reaction window. This combines with an overall correlation of forces in terms of fourth-plus- and fifth-generation aircraft that is not in Russia's favor (see Figure 2.4).

Summary

Our analysis of Russian threat perceptions is summarized in Table 2.1.

Shared Concerns

Unsurprisingly, there are important divergences in NATO and Russian threat perceptions. NATO member states are more concerned about Russian exercises than vice versa, for example. But it is also evident that NATO and Russia share some common areas of concern. These include:

- proximity
- precision-strike capabilities, particularly LRS

---

[35] "Russian Military Experts Downplay Significance of 'Danger' from Mooted F-22 Europe Deployment," *Gazeta.ru*, August 25, 2015.

Figure 2.4
Comparison of NATO and Russian Fourth Generation-Plus Aircraft Holdings (2017 Levels)

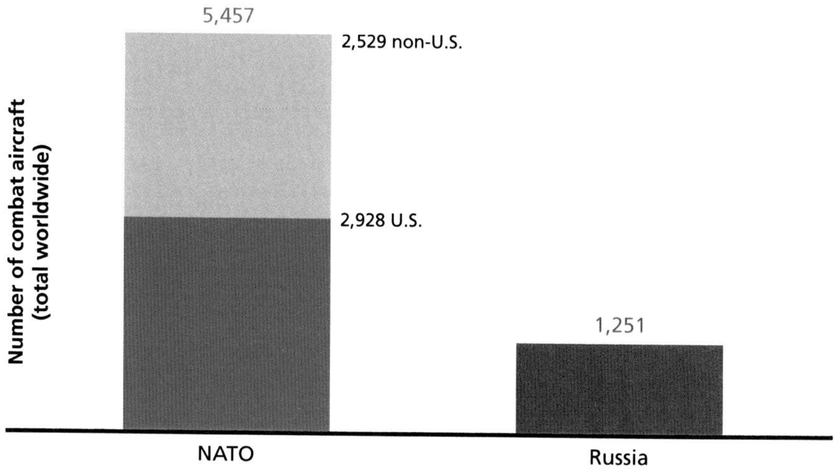

SOURCE: Boston et al., 2018.

Table 2.1
Russian Threat Perceptions

Category of Threat	Specific Threats to Russia
Land domain	• Existence of future large mechanized force (multi-brigade or multi-division) on Russian borders, particularly if supported by theater-wide logistics • Particular Russian geographic vulnerabilities
NATO infrastructure and logistics improvements	• Creation of forward weapons and equipment storage • Buildup of infrastructure to facilitate force flow east
Long-range strike	• Escalatory pressure created by IPW concept and expected NATO aerospace barrage • Presence of air and naval assets with LRS capabilities • BMD ambiguity
Air power	• Early-warning challenge posed by proximity and speed of NATO airpower • Being outnumbered by NATO in fourth-plus- and fifth-generation aircraft

- vulnerable geography and lines of communication (LoCs)
- lack of strategic depth.

Among NATO allies, the nature of the threat posed by Russia is largely determined by geography. States in closer proximity to Russia are more concerned with capabilities that enable short-notice attack, reduce early-warning time, or potentially limit NATO access. Likewise, Russia's threat perceptions are heightened by increased military infrastructure in close proximity to its borders.

Both sides demonstrate shared concerns regarding precision-strike capabilities. From the Russian perspective, NATO's air- and sea-based long-range precision-strike capabilities—and the potential for land-based BMD sites to launch cruise missiles—could be used to deliver considerable kinetic effects and are challenging to trace or counter, creating additional uncertainty that elevates Russia's sense of vulnerability. For NATO, Moscow's extensive strike capabilities from multiple platforms similarly provide Russia with the opportunity to target NATO's critical transport infrastructure or military bases with little or no warning.

Both NATO and Russia share concerns about vulnerabilities of important LoCs. Access to Kaliningrad seems to be an equally important concern for Russia, as is access to the Baltic states across the Suwalki gap for NATO.[36]

A final commonality between NATO and Russia is a shared concern over strategic depth, particularly in the Baltic region. For NATO, the short distance between the Baltic Sea and the borders of the Baltic states with Russia or Belarus essentially deprives the alliance of any strategic depth. On a map, Russia would seem to have an advantage given its vast interior, but, in fact, the location of major population centers and key military bases close to the country's western frontier makes it vulnerable as well. The lack of depth creates concerns about warning time and preemption, and thus could incentivize a first strike in a crisis.

---

[36] The Suwalki gap is a 100-kilometer-wide strip on the Polish-Lithuanian border between Belarus and Kaliningrad, the only land route from Poland to the three Baltic states.

CHAPTER THREE
Conflict Scenarios

This chapter presents four high-level, hypothetical scenario vignettes designed to illustrate various factors that might contribute to conflict initiation or escalation in Europe across the land, air, and maritime domains. All the scenarios take place in 2025, and therefore they incorporate assumptions about capability enhancements both in Russia and in NATO member states. As with our study as a whole, these scenarios focus on conventional military escalation only; escalatory factors arising in the gray zone or above the nuclear threshold were excluded from consideration. The scenarios are not predictions, but are instead intended to highlight the factors that could lead to escalatory dynamics.

The experts who generated the scenarios were asked to work backward from a war that had started in 2025. Similar to World War I, this war was precipitated because of a security dilemma: Both sides were driven by fear of the implications of the other's behavior, and these fears led to an action-reaction escalatory spiral. Fighting broke out when one side perceived an attack as imminent, or believed it would suffer a debilitating change in the military balance if it did not attack first, which led it to order a preemptive strike. The conflict was not the result of premeditated aggression. Neither side intended to start a war, but neither side was willing to moderate its behavior to avoid war.

The first three scenarios address the question of how this war began by outlining the particular steps that led to destabilization. What capabilities were present and how were they postured? Were there specific systems or a combination of systems or capabilities that created incentives for a first strike? What led one or both sides to perceive a need for preemption? To make the analytical task more manageable, we asked three of the scenario-builders to confine the source of escalation in their respective narratives to one of the three conventional military domains—land, air, or maritime. Whereas these three scenarios ended at the point of war initiation, the fourth began at that point to examine what might happen in the first few weeks of combat across the domains.

Scenario One: Escalation in the Land Domain

This scenario begins with Russia conducting a no-notice snap exercise of unprecedented mass in Belarus.[1] Previously, snap exercises had only occurred on Russian territory. The forces engaged in the drill include elements from major ground combat formations, including the First Guards Tank Army. Within three days, two air-assault regiments from the 76th Guards Air Assault division are deployed along the Latvian and Lithuanian borders to participate in the training. Russia insists that, although unprecedented in terms of both location and size, this exercise is purely for training purposes; from NATO's perspective, the posture is consistent with preparations for an offensive into Latvia and Lithuania. Without explanation, Russia curtails passenger rail service in the areas where the exercise is taking place. As part of the exercise, Russia also repositions two regiments of S-400 long-range air-defense systems west, within 100km of the Latvian and Lithuanian borders. Russia publicly maintains that these movements are part of the snap exercise focusing on readiness and training for operational deployment, and should not be viewed by NATO allies as precursors to an invasion. Russia also states that this deployment is no different than the previous deployment of U.S. capabilities to the Baltic states for joint training exercises with NATO allies.

The United States is unconvinced by these pronouncements and regardless believes it should reassure its threatened allies. The U.S.

[1] This scenario was devised by Gian Gentile, senior political scientist at the RAND Corporation, and presented at the project workshop in Berlin, Germany, in January 2019.

president orders U.S. Army units currently stationed in Germany to fall in on prepositioned stocks (APS) and relocate to areas in Poland for training exercises. A U.S. Department of Defense spokesperson states that if the Russians can move major ground forces as part of a training exercise with its allies, then the United States certainly can do the same. On a national basis, other allies also take action. Poland deploys ground forces (16th and 18th Mechanized Infantry Divisions and 18th Reconnaissance Regiment) into tactical fighting positions along its borders with Belarus and Lithuania. The Polish Army also moves its 18th Armored Cavalry Division east toward Warsaw. All three Baltic states also forward deploy parts of their ground combat forces, and Latvia mobilizes three National Guard battalions. All allies stress that these movements are purely for training purposes. The North Atlantic Council declines to mobilize the NATO Response Forces because of a lack of consensus on how to respond to Russia's actions.

In response to the flow of U.S. forces forward and the Polish redeployments, Russia sends additional air-defense and artillery units to reinforce the 1st Guards Tank Army, which has moved closer to the Latvian and Lithuanian borders. Russia also deploys additional medium- and long-range air-defense units to Kaliningrad. The Lithuanian media report sightings of Russian soldiers in Belarus loading live (not training) ammunition onto their tanks and infantry fighting vehicles.

These Russian actions prompt the United States to move most of the ground combat forces that had earlier been redeployed to Poland—one U.S. Army Armored Brigade Combat Team, one Stryker Brigade Combat Team, one Field Artillery Brigade, and a Division Command element—through the Suwalki gap and Lithuania into Latvia. The U.S. president reiterates that this forward movement is primarily for training purposes; however, he also states that these ground forces are also there to show solidarity with NATO allies and will respond to any Russian military move against allied troops or territories. Lead elements of these U.S. ground formations begin to arrive east of Riga in Latvia and establish assembly area positions in coordination with Latvian armed forces.

Shortly after the first U.S. forces arrive in Latvia, a U.S. supply convoy has an accident at a railroad crossing point in Lithuania along the main resupply route heading from Poland to Latvia. This incident is misinterpreted in Moscow as a U.S. attempt to sever the (rail-based) land link with Kaliningrad under the guise of training exercises. To prevent this from happening, Russia fires a salvo from a Tornado-S rocket artillery battery in Kaliningrad, aiming at the location of the U.S. convoy accident. The attack kills two U.S. soldiers and wounds a dozen more. At the same time, U.S. ground troops in Latvia report that their radio-electronic C2 systems are being jammed by Russian helicopter-borne EW systems from across the border. Senior U.S. Army commanders on the ground in Latvia report that these EW attacks might be part of preparations for a Russian offensive.

Scenario Two: Escalation in the Air Domain

This scenario assumes a context of heightened tensions between NATO and Russia, with relations becoming increasingly strained in the years leading up to 2025.[2] Insecurity about possible Russian aggressive intentions causes NATO to increase its deployments and exercises in the Baltic region. In response, Russian air and naval activity in the region becomes increasingly assertive, and snap exercises in the Western Military District are a much more frequent occurrence. In 2024, an increased number of Russian military sorties are flown near the Baltic states' and Sweden's airspace, and NATO allies receive reports of Russian submarine activity in NATO waters. Mock bomb runs by Russian aircraft also take place near the Polish, Baltic, and German coasts.

In January 2025, NATO conducts a winter exercise in Poland and Lithuania, with U.S. forces falling in on an APS in Lithuania. Russia perceives this force flow as a possible threat to Kaliningrad and

---

[2] This scenario was devised by Forrest Morgan, adjunct senior political scientist at the RAND Corporation, and presented at the project workshop in Berlin, Germany, in January 2019.

initiates a snap exercise in Belarus in response. As tensions continue to rise, a Russian Su-30 is shot down after violating Polish airspace while making a mock bomb run on Kolobrzeg Naval Base. The Su-30 was running with friend or foe identification off and did not respond to radio orders from Polish air defense. Moscow terminates the snap exercise in Belarus and deploys the forces mobilized for it to the Lithuanian border near the Suwalki gap. Alarmed by this development, NATO allies agree to mobilize forces and deploy them to defend access to the Baltics. The United States begins preparing to deploy and surge its air capabilities.

On January 15, 2025, U.S. Transportation Command receives the warning order and begins to plan for surge operations. The next day, the deployment order is issued. As the U.S. airlift system prepares to surge, Maritime Sealift Command begins to ready Fast Sealift Ships and large, medium-speed, roll-on/roll-off ships, and fighter and bomber squadrons along with ground forces prepare to deploy from the continental United States. By January 17, the U.S. airlift fleet is at surge level, creating a substantial amount of force moving simultaneously toward Eastern Europe.

Watching as thousands of U.S. forces flow into the Baltic region, Moscow sees a direct threat and believes it must respond. A Russian S-400 shoots down a U.S. C-17 as it is transiting the Baltic en route to Lithuania, with a resulting loss of 135 U.S. personnel; simultaneously, conventionally armed Russian ballistic missiles strike airbases in Lithuania and Poland. Cluster munitions destroy F-35s and A-10s on the parking aprons and unitary munitions crater runways and destroy key facilities. Within the hour, conventionally armed Russian cruise missiles have also struck NATO C2 nodes throughout Lithuania and Poland and, having gained temporary air superiority, Russian air forces launch mass raids on NATO ground forces in Lithuania and Poland. These attacks result in substantial NATO losses.

Scenario Three: Escalation in the Maritime Domain

In the maritime domain, timelines at the operational and strategic levels are slower than in the other domains, presenting greater opportunities to avoid escalation.[3] At the tactical level, single incidents (excluding deliberate attacks) are less likely to lead to broader clashes. Inadvertent escalation, therefore, might be less likely to begin in the maritime domain compared with the other operational environments. However, a combination of simultaneous events, compounded by limited decisionmaking time and lack of a clear operational picture could potentially lead to a clash that spirals into a larger war. Three high-level scenarios are outlined in the following sections, presenting a range of possible circumstances that could provoke conflict in the maritime domain. It should be noted that the scenarios limit themselves to consideration of maritime capabilities operating under NATO, as opposed to individual member-state, command.

Scenario 3a: Red Asymmetry

A NATO warship, part of Standing NATO Maritime Group One, is patrolling in the Baltic Sea. At the same time, a Russian naval formation composed of three surface ships and an attack submarine is also navigating in the same area, sailing from the Gulf of Finland toward Kaliningrad. Russia decides to conduct a snap naval exercise with these assets that involves the use of live missiles and artillery. The NATO warship reports periodic interception of fire-support radar emissions and Russian fighter jets conducting approaches. NATO does not have any information about whether these fighter jets are armed. The NATO warship is then targeted with a sophisticated EW attack, temporarily losing all command, control, communications, computers, and intelligence capabilities. This creates conditions of heightened uncertainty for NATO that, coupled with the concurrent presence of multiple possible threats across the three domains, could trigger a kinetic response.

---

[3] This scenario was devised by Giacomo Persi Paoli, who was at the time associate director for Defense, Security and Infrastructure at RAND Europe, and presented at the project workshop in Berlin, Germany, in January 2019.

Scenario 3b: Blue Asymmetry

The NATO Standing NATO Maritime Group Two is conducting a naval exercise in the Black Sea together with a Ukrainian Navy vessel. During this exercise, a NATO warship detects a Russian attack submarine navigating on the surface close to Romanian territorial waters, which then resubmerges. NATO ships sail in that direction to investigate the contact. Perceiving a possible threat, a Russian naval formation leaves the Black Sea Fleet base at Sevastopol and sails, at speed, toward the last known location of the submarine. In this confined space that limits reaction time, and with both sides uncertain about the other's intentions, a close encounter between the two large naval formations results in a miscalculation or inadvertent incident that leads to a clash.

Scenario 3c: Increased Militarization of the Black Sea

Because of a breakdown in Turkey's relations with other NATO allies, Ankara requests that Moscow enhance its maritime presence in the Black Sea. Russia transfers a number of vessels from the Northern Fleet to the Black Sea Fleet, including ships and submarines armed with *Kalibr* cruise missiles. At the same time, the Azerbaijan-Georgia-Romania Interconnector—intended to bring Azerbaijani gas to Europe by piping the gas to the Georgian Black Sea coast, liquifying it, and shipping it across the Black Sea to be re-gasified in the Romanian port of Constanta—has begun to function. The European Union issues a statement of support and welcomes this development as an important move to boost Europe's energy security.

In the first six months after the Azerbaijan-Georgia-Romania Interconnector comes online, Russian ships begin shadowing and harassing the gas tankers sailing across the Black Sea. At the same time, Russia is also conducting an increased number of no-notice live-fire exercises, targeting areas in close proximity to Romanian territorial waters and the Bosphorus Strait. An additional S-400 air-defense system and more P-800 *Oniks* coastal anti-ship missiles are also deployed to Crimea, providing Russia with almost total coverage of the Black Sea and securing Russia's undisputed military superiority in the area.

Several instances of Global Positioning System spoofing are reported by NATO vessels in the Black Sea, demonstrating Russia's ability to control access to and navigation within the region. Romania is increasingly vocal about the threats to its national security arising from Russia's sea-based capabilities. On one occasion, a Russian warship inadvertently collides with a liquified national gas tanker, causing a massive explosion. This is seen as a deliberate act of aggression by Romania, which launches a kinetic response.

Scenario Four: War in Northern Europe

This scenario outlines one plausible description of how Russian and NATO forces might interact in the early stages of a conflict.[4] The scenario takes place in a context of Russian concerns about the vulnerability of Kaliningrad and NATO worries about the territorial integrity and credibility of the alliance.

In 2025, a large Russian contingent is present in the Western Military District as part of a no-notice snap exercise. This represents Russia's largest snap exercise to date, with the stated goal of enhancing defensive capabilities and guaranteeing the country's security. At the same time, there is a NATO contingent in Latvia as part of an exercise meant to build interoperability and demonstrate alliance cohesion. The NATO forces experience jamming that degrades their communications capabilities as they embark on their drills.

As a NATO supply convoy travels north from Poland through Lithuania to Latvia, a truck carrying munitions accidentally explodes, causing extensive damage to the Varena rail station. Russia interprets this as a deliberate attempt to sever its (rail-based) LoC to Kaliningrad. Russia launches a limited artillery strike that kills two U.S. soldiers. Russia states that it was taking "measured actions" as a protective measure from the perceived NATO threat. Seeing Moscow's actions as a direct attack on alliance territory, the Lithuanian government asks

---

[4] This scenario was devised by Michael Spirtas, senior political scientist at the RAND Corporation, and presented at the project workshop in Berlin, Germany, in January 2019.

NATO for an Article V mutual-defense declaration, and the North Atlantic Council agrees. NATO mobilizes three Armored Brigade Combat Teams and two air wings, bolsters its maritime posture in the Mediterranean, and orders troops in Latvia to move south toward Poland. Polish and other NATO forces move toward the Poland-Belarus border.

At the outbreak of conflict, Russian surface and submarine forces withdraw from the Baltic Sea. NATO surface and submarine forces also draw back, and NATO begins an effort to transport heavy equipment from the United States to Europe via sealift. NATO and Russian surface forces in the Mediterranean stand off from one another, and there is an increase in Russian subsurface, surface, and air activity in the Black Sea.

Russia conducts a large-scale artillery barrage against NATO forces in Latvia; this results in several hundred casualties and destroys many tanks, infantry fighting vehicles, and other equipment. Russian forces then move through Belarus into Lithuania. The 1st Guards Tank Division, reinforced by a Motor Rifle Brigade, moves toward Kaunas along railway lines. The 20th Guards Army moves toward Kaliningrad.

Russian S-300V, S-300PM, and S-400 systems in Kaliningrad and 9K35 *Strela*, 9K38 *Igla*, and S-400s accompanying advancing ground forces target NATO aircraft. NATO responds with air packages, including F-22s and U.S. and Norwegian F-35s, targeting air-defense radars in both locations. NATO loses a large number of aircraft in the air, while Russian air defenses sustain significant damage. The Russian Ministry of Defense issues a statement that it considers attacks on Kaliningrad air defenses to be a significant threat to Russian security.

NATO's Supreme Allied Commander Europe expresses concern that NATO forces in the Baltic states could soon be cut off from their LoCs. Russian ground forces advance into Lithuania, deploying south of the Neris and Nemunas rivers and using artillery and rockets against NATO forces. The 20th Guards Combined Arms Army advances into southern Lithuania toward Kaliningrad and engages Polish forces and U.S. Army fires with artillery and rockets. NATO and Russian air forces are also drawn into confrontation; Kaliningrad IADS selectively engage NATO air packages, with moderate attrition on both sides. The U.S. air bases in Ramstein, Germany and Aviano, Italy are hit by missiles that damage aircraft and temporarily disable runways. The Russian president issues a statement that the allied force must stand down and allow free passage to Kaliningrad or else face "liquidation." Russia is able to establish a land bridge from Belarus to Kaliningrad. The 20th Guards deploys units along the land bridge to guard railways, highways, and other LoCs.

Observations from the Scenarios

To reiterate, these are notional scenarios, not predictions. They are, by definition, artificial and somewhat arbitrary; it is possible to imagine a range of other roads to war and scenarios for early steps in a conflict. We include them here because they help to isolate potentially relevant factors that a CAC regime could address. The next chapter will list those factors. Here, we present some overall observations based on the scenarios themselves:

- Escalation timescales vary between the domains. Force generation that leads to escalation on the ground and on the seas will take considerable time, whereas clashes in the air could spiral more quickly. The land domain was more prone to rapid escalation during the Cold War than it is today because of the huge numbers of forces that were forward deployed on both sides.
- The maritime domain, which played a role in both the air and early-conflict scenarios, figured more prominently than it did during the Cold War. The Fulda gap, the notional locus on the inner-German border of a potential ground war between NATO and the Warsaw Pact, was far from the sea, whereas the current regions of concern are defined by seas (Black Sea and Baltic regions).

- Forward movement of air-defense assets proved escalatory in several cases. A nominally defensive system was perceived as offensive.
- In the scenarios, advanced capabilities in themselves did not necessarily create instability; posturing and signals of intent were equally important.
- Snap exercises were a significant destabilizing factor.
- APS and other prepositioned equipment accelerated the escalation process.
- LoCs are critical, both as assets and liabilities. When the current arms control regimes were negotiated, they were not such a significant problem.
- Unmanned aerial vehicles (UAVs) did not play a role in any of the scenarios. In the workshop discussion, the scenario authors noted that this was not an oversight; UAVs cannot survive in a contested airspace and thus are not relevant in the NATO-Russia context. This is notable because UAVs are frequently mentioned as one of the "new" capabilities that should be included in a future CAC regime.

CHAPTER FOUR

Military Factors That Drive Conflict and Escalation

To process the data presented in the previous two chapters—regarding possible pathways to conflict and escalation—we first distilled the threat perceptions research and the scenarios into discrete escalatory events or actions. For the scenarios, this process entailed disentangling each step on the road to war. The threat perceptions were transformed into a list of actions that were identified as potentially escalatory. These events, in turn, were further disaggregated into what we termed *military factors*: generalizable categories for military dynamics that had an escalatory effect.

See Table 4.1 for an illustration of how we applied this methodology to the land-domain scenario above.

Each cell in the left-hand column contains one of the events in the scenario, beginning with the snap exercise in Belarus and concluding with the accidental explosion of the U.S. supply convoy vehicle. We then developed generic terms to describe why the particular event was escalatory. For example, the snap exercise in Belarus heightened NATO threat perceptions because of the location of the exercise and the massing of forces it entailed. The right-hand column contains the factors invoked by the given event.

By doing the same for all the scenarios and the threat perception data, we arrived at a list of 14 military factors that played a role in conflict initiation or escalation:

Table 4.1
Dissecting the Land-Domain Escalation Scenario

Key Event	Military Factors
Russian snap training exercise in Belarus, with unprecedented mass, in posture that indicates possible preparations for offensive into Latvia and Lithuania	• Training exercises in strategically significant locations • Massing of forces
Positioning of Russian S-400 closer to Latvian and Lithuanian borders	• Training exercises involving new or escalatory capabilities in strategically sensitive locations
Eastward flow of U.S. units in Europe for exercises in forward positions	• Massing of forces • Training exercises in strategically sensitive locations
Deployment of Polish combat divisions on Belarusian and Lithuanian borders	• Military activities, including deployments, in strategically sensitive locations • Massing of forces
Russian deployment of additional artillery and air defense near Latvia and Lithuania, and additional medium-and long-range air defense into Kaliningrad	• Military activities, including deployments, involving new or escalatory capabilities in strategically sensitive locations
Forward movement of U.S. ground combat forces into Latvia, and coordination with Latvian forces, invoking Russian fears of a threat to Kaliningrad land bridge	• Training exercises in strategically sensitive locations • Vulnerable LoCs
Accidental explosion of U.S. supply convoy vehicle	• Ambiguous incident

NOTE: Left-hand column contains the discrete events in the scenario. Right-hand column breaks each event into generic military factors that drove the escalatory dynamic in the scenario.

1. **Military activities, including deployments, in strategically sensitive locations:** Examples include new deployments to border areas or flowing of forces through sensitive areas.
2. **Military activities, including deployments, involving new or escalatory capabilities in strategically sensitive locations:** This is a subset of Factor 1, meant to highlight the escalatory role of deployment of new capabilities—i.e., systems that had not previously been present—to a particular location. In other words, the escalation is a function of the introduction of a particular capability into a particular geography. This action could reduce early-warning time, put key assets at risk, or be seen as a sign of imminent aggression. This factor refers to escalation caused by the inherent qualities of certain capabilities. Important examples include forward positioning or deployment of ground-based air- or maritime-defense systems, forward deployment of stealth aircraft, and prepositioning or forward deployment of ground combat enablers.
3. **Training exercises in strategically sensitive locations:** This factor is also essentially a subset of Factor 1 (e.g., exercises in border areas or other sensitive spots), but because exercises figured so prominently in the scenarios, we separated them from other military activities.
4. **Training exercises involving new or escalatory capabilities in strategically sensitive locations:** This is equivalent to Factor 2, but the introduction of a new capability occurs within the context of an exercise. This factor assumes that the new capability would remain in the area only for the duration of the exercise.
5. **Training exercises involving the use of live fire in the maritime domain:** This factor highlights the escalatory role of live-fire exercises on the seas.
6. **Enhanced readiness:** This factor highlights the escalatory role of either a rapid change of unit or force readiness, expressed in number of hours or days that a given unit needs to be deployed, or an increase in the overall proportion of deployed high-readiness forces.

7. **Massing of forces:** This factor refers to escalation driven by efforts to mass forces. For example, the large Russian snap exercise in Belarus had the effect of causing a large concentration of Russian forces. Of course, the location of the concentration matters, so there will be some overlap here with Factors 1 and 3.
8. **Violations of airspace (or perceived violations):** This factor highlights the escalatory role of airspace violations (real, perceived, or reported) by adversary air assets (e.g., a Russian fighter is believed to stray into NATO airspace or vice versa). For the purposes of this study, this factor refers either to an unintentional violation or a case in which it is unclear whether the violation was intentional.
9. **Violations of maritime borders (or perceived violations):** This factor highlights the escalatory role of violations (real, perceived, or reported) of territorial waters by adversary naval assets (e.g., reports of Russian submarines in NATO territorial waters or vice versa). For the purposes of this study, this factor refers either to an unintentional violation or a case in which it is unclear whether the violation was intentional.
10. **Proximity of forces or capabilities that reduces decisionmaking time:** This factor refers to escalation driven by shorter decisionmaking windows caused by proximity of forces or capabilities of opposing sides. The proximity of opposing forces to one another is the driver of preemption fears that create incentives to strike first. This applies to both the land and sea domains.
11. **Long-range strike deployment that puts sensitive areas at risk:** This factor refers to a new deployment of precision-guided missiles (land-, sea-, or air-based) that puts key adversary military or civilian targets at risk.
12. **Threats to vulnerable lines of communication:** This factor refers to escalatory pressure created by a perceived imminent threat to the security of land or sea LoCs. Kaliningrad and the Suwalki gap figured prominently in the scenarios.
13. **Ambiguous incident:** This factor refers to a kinetic or near-kinetic event that occurs (particularly at a time of heightened tensions) and it is unclear which party is responsible, the extent

of intentionality, and even how the incident occurred. This factor assumes that existing crisis communication mechanisms do not provide adequate clarity about the incident. An example would be the explosion of the U.S. supply convoy vehicle in the ground scenario.

14. **Lack of transparency regarding capabilities:** This factor refers to one side escalating based on worst-case assumptions because of a lack of transparency regarding a particular capability. For example, a party is forced to assume that forward-deployed fighter jets are armed because it has no evidence to suggest the opposite.

This list is not meant to be a comprehensive accounting of all possible escalatory military factors between NATO and Russia. However, it does account for the vast majority of the factors we were able to distill from the two strands of research described in the previous chapters, and all of the factors that appear multiple times. Therefore, these are the general categories of military factors that a potential future European CAC regime should address. They are presented at a high level of abstraction here, divorced from all context. As an analytical tool, however, this approach allows for isolation of the key conventional military dynamics that could drive a potential conflict.

The list of factors points to two important differences from the circumstances of the Cold War–era military standoff that led to the CFE treaty. First, over half of the listed factors are location-specific. Although CFE did have a number of provisions that were devised for particular locations, most prominently the flank zones, its core provisions were ceilings on national holdings of equipment, which were largely agnostic to location. The factors we have identified suggest that the location of military activities is much more central to possible contingencies than overall conventional capabilities or equipment holdings. In other words, where deployments, activities, and exercises occur is far more likely to be the cause of potential instability than when CFE was negotiated. The centrality of location should be underscored because it suggests the need to depart from the core focus on ceilings found in both CFE and A/CFE. Second, force size and overall force structure were not raised in either the threat perceptions or the scenarios, and therefore are not featured in the list of factors. In the 1980s, NATO pursued CAC because of concerns that Warsaw Pact conventional forces far outnumbered NATO's and were structured and postured for an offensive attack. Although one could identify certain imbalances today, neither side views them as destabilizing. Neither NATO nor Russia see the other as postured for an offensive operation—at least, as of this writing. In other words, current deployments are not destabilizing in themselves. Fears of first-strike surprise attacks, as of today, do not seem pervasive.

These divergences suggest some broad central parameters for future measures. First, such measures must be designed around the particular geography that is the source of potential instability. Continent-wide measures are unlikely to address the core drivers of instability effectively. Second, the locations that are the source of potential instability do not appear to be fixed—they could shift with changes in posture, capabilities, or deployments. A future regime should therefore incorporate a degree of flexibility to accommodate this reality. Third, future CAC measures that go beyond transparency measures should be constraints, not limits on force structure. Former RAND scholars Richard Darilek and John Setear usefully define *constraints* as "measures directly limiting or prohibiting current or future operations by conventional military forces."[1] They contrast constraints with force-structure measures, which include the destruction of equipment, the prohibition of new capabilities, or the elimination of units. These steps could have an impact on operations, but only indirectly. Constraints, by contrast, directly affect operations by, for example, "prescribing the zones of deployment for military forces, the times and conditions under which those forces can exercise, or the degree of acceptable change to their training or operational status."[2] They are thus better suited to the drivers of conflict identified previously.

---

1 Richard E. Darilek and John Setear, *Arms Control Constraints for Conventional Forces in Europe*, N-3046-OSD, Santa Monica, Calif.: RAND Corporation, March 1990, p. 3.

2 Darilek and Setear, 1990, p. 3.

CHAPTER FIVE

Linking Factors to Measures: A Menu

After isolating the military factors central to potential conflict and escalation, we sought to identify CAC measures that *could* be relevant to addressing those factors. We did so through a review of existing treaties and agreements, an examination of the literature on CAC, and a second structured workshop with CAC experts in Berlin. For that workshop, each invited expert was given a subset of the 14 factors in advance and was asked to propose potential measures to address them.[1] (Each of the 14 factors was covered by at least one presenter.) Some—but not all—of their suggestions have been included in this chapter; we chose among them based on the discussion at the workshop, our review of the CAC literature, and our own analytical judgement. We also added our own suggestions for measures using the literature review, the history of implementation of existing agreements, and proposals made but not adopted at previous CAC negotiations.

The measures are presented as a menu of options for consideration rather than a set of recommendations. We did not take into account questions of political feasibility, ease of verification, or strategic desirability. The measures are formulated here at the same level of abstrac-

---

[1] These experts included William Alberque, director of NATO's Arms Control, Disarmament and WMD Non-Proliferation Centre; Ulrich Kühn, head of the Arms Control and Emerging Technologies Program at the Institute for Peace Research and Security Policy at the University of Hamburg; Andrei Zagorski, director of the Department of Arms Control and Conflict Resolution Studies at the Primakov Institute of World Economy and International Relations of the Russian Academy of Sciences; Nicholas Williams, senior associate fellow for the European Leadership Network; and one Polish expert who wished to remain anonymous.

tion as the factors; they are not adapted to the specifics of the Russia-NATO context.

Description of Possible Measures

1. Military activities, including deployments, in strategically sensitive locations:
   a. *Limitations on permanently based forces or infrastructure (including storage sites) in the designated sensitive locations.* These limitations could be in terms of absolute numbers of troops or certain types of equipment—presumably based on what could be used in a cross-border attack—or specifically crafted around counter-concentration in sensitive areas, particularly near borders. For example, a counter-concentration measure could limit the percentage of a state's forces from being stationed within a certain distance of its borders.[2] For the purposes of complicating cross-border operations, the numbers of fixed-wing aircraft, attack helicopters, combat vehicles, or ground-based short-range missiles could be limited.[3]
      i. *Limits on the types of units or numbers of certain units permitted to be permanently based in sensitive locations.* For example, high-readiness forces could be capped or banned from such locations.
   b. *Bans or limits on permanent deployments of enablers required for surprise attack, such as tactical fuelers, air defense, combat bridges, or EW capabilities within the zone.*[4] Instead of limiting equipment or force numbers, these measures would

---

[2] John E. Peters, *CFE and Military Stability in Europe*, Santa Monica, Calif.: RAND Corporation, MR-911-OSD, 1997, p. 34.

[3] Gregory G. Govan, "Conventional Arms Control in Europe: Overcome by Events, or New Perspectives?" *Security and Human Rights*, Vol. 26, 2015a, p. 85.

[4] Peters, 1997, p. 39.

complicate the ability to carry out cross-border operations of any size without warning.

c. *Restrictions on colocation of enablers and related capabilities that are required for surprise attack or cross-border operations within the zone.* For example, in the zone, heavy-equipment transporters would not be allowed to be permanently stationed with tanks.[5] Such a measure would reduce the ability to rapidly forward deploy the tanks without reducing their defensive capacity.
d. *Limitations on codeployment of certain units to minimize offensive capability of permanently stationed forces within the zone.* For example, the number of combat engineering companies permanently associated with any maneuver unit in the zone could be limited. Similarly, the number of artillery battalions in support of a maneuver unit could be limited.[6]
e. *Limitations on size of temporary additional deployments in sensitive locations.* These measures would either prevent or limit the size of deployments beyond an agreed baseline for a particular sensitive location to prevent a concentration of forces there.
f. *Rather than limitations, a measure could consist of commitments regarding the size or nature of potential future deployments in the sensitive area.* For example, states could commit to deploying no greater than a certain number of a given category of equipment in the zone.
g. *Limitations on out-of-garrison activities of permanently stationed forces within the sensitive area.* To complicate surprise attack, the forces permanently stationed within the designated area, for example, could be prevented from movement beyond a certain radius (with exceptions for rotation and training).
h. *Notification-threshold requirements for deployments or other activities in sensitive locations.* In addition to the constrain-

5 Peters, 1997, p. 39.

6 Peters, 1997, p. 36.

ing measures mentioned above, parties could be obliged to notify one another new or temporary deployments in the zone or other activities in advance. For example, there could be a required month-in-advance notification before temporarily stationing units within a certain distance of a designated border. This measure could also apply to specified sensitive maritime zones.

i. *Enhanced information exchanges on forces permanently stationed within the specified area.* These would include detail on forces, equipment, and reinforcement infrastructure, including headquarters and prepositioned equipment.

2. Military activities, including deployments, involving new or escalatory capabilities in strategically sensitive locations:
   a. *Bans or limits on deployments of specified capabilities in designated sensitive areas, except in the context of notified exercises.* For example, air-defense systems or stealth aircraft could be prohibited from being stationed in a given zone.
   b. *Notification requirements for deployments of specified capabilities or activities involving specified capabilities in sensitive locations.* For example, LRS-capable ships entering the Black or Baltic Seas could be subject to notification.

3. Training exercises in strategically sensitive locations:
   a. *Ban or limit on number of exercises in sensitive locations.* For example, a party could be allowed two exercises per year in a given zone (including maritime).
   b. *Limit on size of exercises in sensitive locations.* Exercises involving more than a specified number of troops or pieces of equipment could be prohibited in the specified sensitive location.
   c. *Limit on duration of exercises in sensitive locations.* To prevent preparation for operations from taking place under the cover of exercises, the events in the zones could be limited to a certain number of days—long enough to allow for training, but not long enough to launch a cross-border attack.

d. *Ban or limit on number of no-notice exercises in sensitive locations.* To address concerns about so-called snap exercises, such exercises could either be completely banned or strictly limited in number within a sensitive zone.
e. *Limit on the size of no-notice exercises in sensitive locations.* No-notice exercises that are allowed in the zone could be limited in size.
f. *Limit on total number of troops involved in parallel exercises in sensitive zones.* Russia has taken advantage of the VDoc loophole that allows parties to declare multiple parallel exercises to stay below the threshold for inspection. A new measure for sensitive locations could address this loophole by regulating the total number of troops involved in parallel exercises within the zone. The allowed number could be equivalent to the limit for temporary deployments in the sensitive location.
g. *Establishment of a minimum time period between single exercises in sensitive locations.* In order to minimize the threatening nature of exercises, a minimum of a certain number of days between separate training events could be established.
h. *No threshold for observation and notification of exercises in sensitive locations.* Regardless of which constraints are adopted, parties could be required to notify one another of all exercises in the zones and invite observers.
i. *Additional provisions for naval exercise observation and notification in sensitive zones.* Naval exercises have traditionally been excluded from CSBM agreements. However, a measure could provide for mandatory notification and possibly observation of all naval exercises in specified sensitive zones.
j. *Limitations or voluntary commitments on the number of naval vessels participating in joint maritime-land-air exercises.* Exercises involving all three domains are potentially the most escalatory. Parties could restrict the number of naval vessels that participate within the zone.

4. Training exercises involving new or escalatory capabilities in strategically sensitive locations:
   a. *Limit on which capabilities can be used in exercises in strategically sensitive locations.* For example, attack helicopters could be prohibited from taking part in training events in the zones.

5. Training exercises involving the use of live fire in the maritime domain:
   a. *Live-fire exercises limited to pre-agreed naval ranges.* For example, in the Baltic, Black, and Mediterranean Seas, specified areas for live-fire naval exercises could be designated. Outside of those areas, no live-fire training would be permitted.
   b. *Enhanced notification or observation requirements for naval exercises involving live fire.* Lower thresholds for advance notification and invitation of observers.

6. Enhanced readiness:
   a. *Agreed definitions of* readiness *and regular exchange of additional data.* Any measures to address readiness must be based on a shared definition of the term. Parties then would need to share a degree of information regarding units that could be considered "high-readiness."
   b. *Notification mechanisms for enhanced readiness of forces.*
      i. Prior notification could be required for moving units not designated as high-readiness to such a state.
      ii. Temporary deployment of those units designated as high-readiness could be subject to advance notification.
   c. *Limitations on overall readiness.* The proportion of a nation or bloc's forces kept at high readiness could be limited.[7]
   d. *Notification requirements for movements of high-readiness forces.* Designated high-readiness forces could be subject to

---

7 Davis, 1988, p. 59.

additional notification requirements when they move out of garrison for whatever reason.

7. Massing of forces:
   a. *Regular information exchange on deployments.* To provide a common baseline for understanding what *massing* means, there would need to be enhanced information shared on normal, peacetime force levels. *Massing* should be precisely defined in terms of a departure from that norm.
   b. *Measures to prevent concentration of forces along borders.* Limits on the percentage of a state's forces permitted to be deployed temporarily within a certain distance of its borders could curtail the possibility of concentration.
   c. *Notification of plans to mass forces.* For example, parties could commit to providing advance notification of plans for temporary deployments to another country that would increase overall numbers of forces in a given country over a certain percentage of the declared numbers. Within a given country, there could be a notification threshold for exceeding a certain percentage of forces located within a certain distance of the border.
   d. *Measures to complicate rapid concentration of forces.*
      i. *A cap on the number of assembled railcars in any one railyard.* Because much movement of military units in Europe occurs by rail, such a limit would make concentration of forces more difficult. John Peters suggested a cap of 1,000 flatcars per railyard. Such a step would restrict the size of a force that could be moved from a single point. He also suggested advance notification requirements for assembling more than 450 flatcars to deploy a brigade for exercises or other activities.[8]
      ii. *Limitations on permanent fuel storage at dispersal airfields and notification requirements before establishing temporary*

---

[8] Peters, 1997, p. 38.

fuel storage at such airfields. Dispersal airfields would be used only to move large quantities of forces.[9]

iii. *Notification period before assembling more than four roll-on/roll-off ships and more than four break-bulk ships.* These vessels are only required for large sea-based deployments.[10]

e. *Limitation on number of units that can be out of garrison at any time.*[11] By definition, this measure would prevent massing.

8. Violations of airspace (or perceived violations):
   a. *Creation of Nuclear Risk Reduction Center (NRRC)–like nodes for crisis communications.* The NRRCs in Moscow and Washington were created in 1988 as a bilateral mechanism for transmitting treaty-based notifications and for crisis communications between the United States and the Soviet Union.[12] NRRCs are staffed around the clock. Similar nodes could be created in all relevant capitals to ensure effective crisis communications. Alternatively, a node could be established at NATO Headquarters or Supreme Headquarters, Allied Powers Europe and in Moscow to avoid overburdening individual allied governments.[13]
   b. *Creation of a special standing consultative body to address incidents.* Holding regularly scheduled meetings of Russian and NATO officials and military officers to discuss *ex post* particular incidents could be useful as a preventative measure

---

[9] Peters, 1997, p. 39.

[10] Peters, 1997, p. 39.

[11] This idea is suggested in Gregory G. Govan, "Conventional Arms Control in Europe: Some Thoughts About an Uncertain Future," *Deep Cuts Issue Brief*, No. 5, July 2015b, p. 2.

[12] See U.S. Department of State, *United States Nuclear Risk Reduction Center (NRRC)*, Washington, D.C., 2012.

[13] The NATO-Russia Cooperative Airspace Initiative set an important precedent for this kind of mechanism, albeit in the civilian domain.

to reduce misunderstanding. The NATO-Russia Council could be an appropriate venue.

c. *Creation of an updated, multilateral Prevention of Dangerous Military Activities Agreement (PDMA).* The existing PDMAs, which the United States, Canada, Greece, and the Czech Republic have with Russia on a bilateral basis, have provisions that lay out procedures for operating near the territory of the other party and establish radio frequencies and signals to communicate directly. The extent to which these bilateral agreements are being implemented today is unclear. In the U.S. case, there has not been a meeting of the joint implementation commission since 1990. A new measure or agreement on dangerous activities could be negotiated among all the relevant parties to establish crisis communication mechanisms to clarify any perceived airspace violations.

9. Violations of maritime borders (or perceived violations):
   a. *Creation of NRRC-like nodes for crisis communications.* See 8a.
   b. *Creation of a special standing consultative body to address incidents.* See 8b.
   c. *Establish standalone, multilateral NATO-Russia Incidents at Sea Agreement (INCSEA).* Such an agreement could designate communication channels and signals for ship-to-ship and ship-to-shore interaction that could effectively serve a hotline function. Currently, the United States, the United Kingdom, Germany, France, Italy, Norway, Spain, the Netherlands, Canada, Portugal, Greece, and Turkey (12 allies in total) have agreements with Russia on incidents at sea. All have very similar provisions that amount to CSBMs. Although there is a case for maintaining separate bilateral INCSEA agreements for states with global navies, it is probably sensible to create a NATO-Russia INCSEA that would apply to all allied vessels in the Baltic, Black, and Mediterranean Seas. Practically, it probably would be easier for

Russian naval officers to operate from a single set of signals rather than 12 different ones. In addition, many of these agreements date from the Cold War; the new consolidated agreement could be both updated and strengthened.[14] A new agreement could also build on a 2014 U.S.-China agreement on incident prevention.[15]

10. Proximity of forces or capabilities that reduces decisionmaking time:
    a. *Measure to ensure that naval vessels maintain a certain distance.* In the scenarios above, escalation in the maritime domain often was a function of the proximity of ships. Such proximity could prove escalatory no matter where the proximity occurs. A provision in the proposed multilateral INCSEA (9c) could be designed to require that ships maintain adequate distance from one another.
    b. *Measures that fall under Factor 1 would likely address proximity in the land domain.*

11. Long-range strike deployment that puts sensitive areas at risk:
    a. *Numerical ceilings on holdings of long-range PGMs.* LRS capabilities are perhaps the only capabilities discussed in this study that are not tied to subregional dynamics and, therefore, are the only capabilities that might be suited to CFE-like ceilings on national holdings. There are, of course, a number of challenges associated with establishing such a

[14] For a detailed proposal to this effect, see Łukasz Kulesa, Thomas Frear, and Denitsa Raynova, *Managing Hazardous Incidents in the Euro-Atlantic Area: A New Plan of Action*, London, UK: European Leadership Network, November 2016. See also Ian Anthony, *Reducing Military Risk in Europe*, Stockholm, Sweden: Stockholm International Peace Research Institute, SIPRI Policy Paper 51, June 2019, pp. 20–35.

[15] U.S. Department of Defense and Ministry of National Defense of the People's Republic of China, "Memorandum of Understanding Between the Department of Defense of the United States of America and the Ministry of National Defense of the People's Republic of China Regarding the Rules of Behavior for Safety of Air and Maritime Encounters," Washington, D.C., and Beijing, China, November 9–10, 2014.

ceiling given that PGMs are land-, air-, and sea-based and can be used in other theaters besides Europe.

b. *Geographical restrictions on deployment of long-range strike capabilities.* For example, a 2,000-km zone extending from Moscow to Berlin could be established in which only a certain number of long-range PGMs could be deployed, either permanently or temporarily. Such restrictions could apply only to land- and sea-based PGMs, because air-launched missiles pose less of a surprise or preemptive strike concern.

c. *Measures that increase time needed to strike.* For example, ground-based launchers could be physically separated from the missiles they fire by a large enough distance to complicate a surprise attack.

d. *Regular declarations regarding PGMs.* Information could be exchanged regarding holdings, deployment sites, or storage sites.

e. *Notification requirements specific to PGMs.* For example, naval vessels entering the Black or Baltic Seas that are armed with PGMs could be subject to prenotification requirements. Movement of road-mobile PGMs and temporary deployments of airframes with PGM capabilities could also be subject to notification.

12. Threats to vulnerable lines of communication:

    a. *For the land domain, the vulnerability of LoCs could be reduced by designing the sensitive zones around them.*

13. Ambiguous incident:

    a. *Creation of NRRC-style communication nodes among all relevant states.* This mechanism would also be relevant for such incidents.

    b. *Creation of an updated, multilateral PDMA.* See 8c.

14. Lack of transparency regarding capabilities:

    a. *Obligatory demonstration procedures for new weapon systems.* Parties could commit to demonstrating newly fielded capabilities to avoid misperceptions. These could be adapted from the New START treaty provisions for demonstration of new types of strategic weapons.

b. *OST 2.0 or persistent shared surveillance.* OST was not designed to be responsive to particular short-term transparency concerns, but the core concept of shared surveillance flights can be adapted for the purposes of an updated CAC regime. To enhance transparency, the parties to a new agreement could create a suite of shared surveillance mechanisms that do not require on-site inspection, such as shared satellites, shared drones, centralized data feeds, and common radar tracking mechanisms.

Table 5.1 demonstrates how we developed the menu of measures using a sample of three events chosen at random from the different scenarios and threat perceptions. The table demonstrates how each measure is ultimately derived from our research on potential sources of escalation.

Table 5.1
How the Menu Was Developed

	Source Material		
	Scenario 1: Ground Escalation	**Threat Perceptions: Russia**	**Scenario 3a: Maritime Escalation**
Key event	Russian snap training exercise in Belarus, with unprecedented mass, in posture that indicates possible preparations for offensive into Latvia and Lithuania	Long-range strike–capable surface vessels within strike range of Russia	Russian use of live fire in naval exercise, in close proximity to NATO warships
Military factor(s)	• Training exercises in strategically sensitive locations • Massing of forces	• Long-range strike deployment that puts sensitive areas at risk	• Training exercises involving the use of live fire
Proposed CAC measure(s)	• 3a: Ban or limit on number of short-notice exercises in sensitive locations • 3b: Limit on the size of short-notice exercises in sensitive locations • 7b: Measures to prevent concentration of forces along borders	• 2b: Notification requirements for deployments of specified capabilities or activities involving specified capabilities in sensitive locations • 11e: Notification requirements specific to PGMs	• 5a: Live-fire exercises limited to pre-agreed naval ranges • 5b: Enhanced notification or observation requirements for naval exercises involving live fire

CHAPTER SIX

Conclusion

Policy Considerations

Developing an agreement from the menu provided in Chapter Five will invoke a number of policy considerations. These considerations were not directly within the scope of this report, but given their importance to discussions on the future of CAC, we list them here:

- **Relationship to existing agreements:** Any negotiations on a new CAC agreement would have to be premised on an understanding of the fate of the existing regime and the relationship of the new agreement to that regime.
- **Membership:** The measures discussed here are aimed at a subset of OSCE participating states, specifically Russia, Russia's allies, and NATO member states. By definition, that would leave a number of states-parties to CFE out of the agreement. However, it should be noted that none of the three existing CAC agreements (CFE, VDoc, and OST) has the same set of parties. Nonetheless, this will be a political challenge. One option could be to create an OSCE-wide framework umbrella agreement that allows for specific measures to be negotiated among subsets of parties, and to nest the proposed NATO-Russia measures within that umbrella framework agreement.
- **Challenges of defining strategically sensitive locations:** The menu in Chapter Five was deliberately silent on how to define

strategically sensitive locations for the location-specific measures. Existing location-specific arms control agreements and measures do not offer a ready-made template for the NATO-Russia circumstances of today. For example, the so-called Five-Party Agreements among Russia, China, Kyrgyzstan, Kazakhstan, and Tajikistan define a zone of application of 100 km on either side of the former Sino-Soviet border. Such a blunt instrument would not be appropriate for the current NATO-Russia frontiers. In all likelihood, the measures would have to be tailor-made to the specific sensitive locations identified; they are unlikely to be symmetrical in terms of depth, particularly in the Baltic context. Such asymmetry is not new for CAC; CFE zones created obligations on certain states that did not apply to others. Due consideration should be given to avoiding rigid zones, such as the CFE flanks, that cannot adapt to changing circumstances. Otherwise, as with CFE, disagreements over the zones can doom the entire regime. As the former senior U.S. CAC negotiator BG (ret.) Gregory Govan notes, "CFE may be fairly stated to have died of complications from sub-national limits."[1]

- **Symmetry no longer relevant:** To a certain extent, even CFE was asymmetrical in terms of the different levels of reductions required of the parties. However, the treaty's overall objective of a conventional balance suggested a degree of desired symmetry. A new CAC agreement will have to dispense with any pretense of symmetry in terms of the impact of measures on the states party to it. The security challenges differ dramatically across the continent, and CAC measures must reflect that diversity to be relevant.
- **Linking location-specific measures into a broader regime:** Given the nature of the NATO alliance, it would not be feasible or desirable to have a CAC regime to which not all allies were party. Therefore, location-specific measures affecting only certain allies will need to be part of a broader agreement involving all allies; standalone border-area measures would not be viable. Compliance concerns, even those involving only two states that

[1] Govan, 2015a, p. 82.

share a border, would have to be dealt with in a consultative body where all parties were present.

- **Moving beyond CFE's five categories:** CFE was centered around the five categories of treaty-limited equipment: tanks, artillery, armored combat vehicles, helicopters, and attack aircraft. These five categories are still central to ground operations and most likely would play a role in the measures described previously. But rather than adding to the five categories, any new CAC agreement should avoid fixed categories of treaty-limited equipment altogether. By their very nature, the different measures described in Chapter Five would apply to different sets of capabilities.
- **Verification and inspection challenges:** A violation of a given measure should provide a high degree of political and military warning. As Darilek and Setear wrote, "the clear violation of a legally agreed-upon constraint speaks volumes about the intentions of the violating party and thus, if nothing else, encourages a response from the other party to the agreement."[2] Measures should create clear criteria for judging behavior and determining violations. Almost all of the measures in Chapter Five would pose novel challenges for verification and inspection. Arms control need not require strict verification—the Presidential Nuclear Initiatives on nonstrategic nuclear weapons are an example—but given the mistrust among the parties, it would be beneficial to have robust verification procedures to enhance confidence and create a mechanism for interaction among the parties' militaries.
- **National versus multinational inspection teams:** Several experts have proposed using a multinational inspection body instead of national inspection teams in a future CAC agreement. Govan, for example, proposes using the International Atomic Energy Agency's Safeguards monitoring procedures as a model.[3] Each approach has its benefits and drawbacks.
- **Linkages to other arms control negotiations:** The original CFE negotiations were conducted on the heels of the successful con-

[2] Darilek and Setear, 1990, p. 22.

[3] Govan, 2015a, p. 86.

clusion of the Intermediate-Range Nuclear Forces Treaty (INF) and in parallel with the Strategic Arms Reduction Treaty talks. These processes positively reinforced one another. A future negotiation on CAC inevitably will be affected by other arms control discussions as well. More specifically, any INF follow-on discussions would directly determine the remit for future CAC talks to address the PGM issue.

- **Maritime arms control challenges:** There were extensive discussions about naval arms control and CSBMs in the 1980s and early 1990s in the context of the talks that led to CFE and the predecessor of VDoc.[4] The maritime domain was ultimately excluded from VDoc, CFE and A/CFE. NATO and the United States, in particular, have long objected to any measures that could be construed as limiting freedom of navigation. However, INCSEA-like measures involving enhanced crisis communication, rules of the road, observation of certain activities, and prenotification have been successfully negotiated and implemented without impinging on freedom of navigation. The maritime domain presents unique challenges for arms control, but these can be overcome given sufficient mutual interest.
- **Avoiding additional pressures on military budgets:** Unlike CFE, the CAC measures proposed here will not drastically reduce forces and thus will not entail significant budgetary savings. Although these measures could reduce subregional arms-race dynamics, which could entail modest efficiencies, that is unlikely to be a major selling point. Therefore, the measures themselves should avoid creating additional economic burdens through implementation of notification, inspection, and verification provisions.

[4] For background on these issues, see James L. Lacy, *The Baroque Debate: Public Diplomacy and Naval Arms Control, 1986-1989*, Santa Monica, Calif.: RAND Corporation, N-3121-USDP, 1990a; James L. Lacy, *Naval Arms Control: The Backdrop of History*, Santa Monica, Calif.: RAND Corporation, N-3120-USDP, 1990b; and James L. Lacy, *Within and Beyond Naval Confidence-Building: The Legacy and the Options*, Santa Monica, Calif.: RAND Corporation, N-3122-USDP, 1991.

Implications

This report presents both an examination of the potential drivers of Russia-NATO conflict and a menu of CAC measures that might address those drivers. The threat perception and scenarios research suggest that there are indeed several conventional military capability– and posture-driven pathways to conflict. These pathways are far more diverse than was the case in the 1980s, leaving us with 14 military factors that contribute to escalatory dynamics, as described in Chapter Four. CAC measures for each of these 14 are suggested in Chapter Five.

The menu of measures is not intended to be a proto-agreement. Each of the proposed measures would have to be adapted from its current context-free form to specific geographic, political-military, and military-technical circumstances. Moreover, negotiating an agreement is not akin to choosing from a menu at a restaurant; there will have to be tradeoffs in any negotiation based on the interests of the other parties at the table.

But the purpose of this study was not to anticipate the outcome of a negotiation. Instead, it was to examine whether there are CAC measures that, if agreed and implemented, could have a significant positive impact on European security. The research presented here suggests that an agreement incorporating measures from the menu could reduce the risk of conflict through misunderstanding or miscalculation and lower escalatory pressures in the early stages of a conflict, were one to occur. Such an agreement could increase warning and decisionmaking time and complicate a surprise attack by making preparation for any offensive action more conspicuous, lengthy, and observable. In other words, this report demonstrates that NATO allies have an interest in considering a new CAC regime because it could produce meaningful security benefits. The menu is meant to inform future intra-alliance and, eventually, NATO-Russia discussions on CAC.

Currently, the debate on this issue at the governmental level tends to begin and end with the existing regimes and the disputes surrounding them. There is no venue for discussing what problems a new CAC regime might address and which measures might be useful to include in such a regime. The lack of such a dialogue is a recipe for policy stasis.

Given the growing military tensions in Europe, in the future there is likely to be a strong demand signal from the political level for new ideas on CAC. When that signal arrives, interested governments should have well-considered proposals ready. Hopefully, this report will help spark a process to produce such proposals.

References

Aksenov, O. Yu., Yu. N. Tretyakov, and Ye. N. Filin, "Osnovnye printspipy sozdaniya sistemy otsenki tekushego i prognoznogo usherba vazhneishim ob'ektam sistemy strategicheskogo sderznivaniya," *Voennaya mysl'*, No. 6, 2015.

Anthony, Ian, *Reducing Military Risk in Europe*, Stockholm, Sweden: Stockholm International Peace Research Institute, SIPRI Policy Paper 51, June 2019.

Antonov, Anatolii, and Rodion Ayumov, *Kontrol' nad obychnymi vooruzheniyami v Evrope—Konets rezhima ili istoriya s prodolzheniem?* Moscow: PIR Center, 2012.

Belobrov, Yurii, "Nadezhdy evropeitsev po vozrozhdeniyu deistvennogo KOVE eshche ne ugasli," *Mezhdunarodnaya zhizn'*, No. 6, 2017.

Boston, Scott, Michael Johnson, Nathan Beauchamp-Mustafaga, and Yvonne K. Crane, *Assessing the Conventional Force Imbalance in Europe: Implications for Countering Russian Local Superiority*, Santa Monica, Calif.: RAND Corporation, RR-2402, 2018. As of December 27, 2019:
https://www.rand.org/pubs/research_reports/RR2402.html

"Bridge from Hellas. Vladimir Putin Visits Athens and the Holy Mountain of Athos," *Rossiiskaya Gazeta*, May 30, 2016.

Brustlein, Corentin, *The Erosion of Strategic Stability and the Future of Arms Control in Europe*, Paris, France: Institut français des relations internationales, IFRI Proliferation Papers, No. 60, November 2018.

Buzhinskiy, Evgeny, and Oleg Shakirov, *Outlines for Future Conventional Arms Control in Europe: A Sub-Regional Regime in the Baltics*, London, UK: European Leadership Network, September 2019.

Center for Strategic and International Studies Missile Defense Project, "JASSM / JASSM ER (AGM-158A/B)," webpage, last updated June 15, 2018. As of January 16, 2020:
https://missilethreat.csis.org/missile/jassm/

———, "Tomahawk," webpage, last updated November 4, 2019. As of December 27, 2019: https://missilethreat.csis.org/missile/tomahawk/

Chekinov, S. G., and S. A. Bogdanov, "Nachalnyye periody voin i ikh vliyanie na podgotovku strany k voine budushchego," *Voennaya mysl'*, No. 11, 2012.

Darilek, Richard E., and John Setear, *Arms Control Constraints for Conventional Forces in Europe*, Santa Monica, Calif.: RAND Corporation, N-3046-OSD, March 1990. As of January 16, 2020:
https://www.rand.org/pubs/notes/N3046.html

Davis, Paul K., *Toward a Conceptual Framework for Operational Arms Control in Europe's Central Region*, Santa Monica, Calif.: RAND Corporation, R-3704-USDP, 1988. As of January 16, 2020:
https://www.rand.org/pubs/reports/R3704.html

Defense Intelligence Agency, *Russia Military Power: Building a Military to Support Great Power Aspirations*, Washington, D.C., 2017.

Durkalec, Jacek, "Rethinking Conventional Arms Control in Europe: A Transparency-Centered Approach," *Strategic File*, No. 7 (34), Polish Institute of International Affairs, September 2013.

Engvall, Johan, Gudrun Persson (ed.), Robert Dalsjö, Carolina Vendil Pallin, and Mike Winnerstig, *Conventional Arms Control: A Way Forward or Wishful Thinking?* Stockholm, Sweden: Swedish Defence Research Agency, FOI-R--4586--SE, April 2018.

Falkenrath, Richard, *Shaping Europe's Military Order: The Origins and Consequences of the CFE Treaty*, Cambridge, Mass.: MIT Press, 1995.

Fedotov, I. A., "Tendentsii razvitiya operativno-strategicheskogo komandovaniya voennogo okruga na sovremennom etape formirovaniya Vooruzhennykh Sil Rossiiskoi Federatsii," *Vestnik AVN*, No. 4, 2016.

Flanagan, Stephen J., and Irina A. Chindea, *Russia, NATO, and Black Sea Security Strategy: Regional Perspectives from a 2019 Workshop*, Santa Monica, Calif.: RAND Corporation, CF-405-OSD, 2019. As of December 19, 2019:
https://www.rand.org/pubs/conf_proceedings/CF405.html

Gerasimov, V., "Generalnii shtab i oborona strany," *Voenno-promyshlennyi kur'er*, February 3, 2014.

Goncharov, A. M., "Voina budet vestis vo vsekh sredakh," *Vozdushno-Kosmicheskaya Oborona*, No. 6, 2015.

Gordon, Michael R., and Vivian Salama, "Trump Moves Closer to Ending Another Post-Cold War Treaty," *Wall Street Journal*, October 27, 2019.

Gottemoeller, Rose, "Revitalizing Security Cooperation in Europe," speech delivered at the Moscow Conference on International Security, Moscow, Russia, May 23, 2013.

Govan, Gregory G., "Conventional Arms Control in Europe: Overcome by Events, or New Perspectives?" *Security and Human Rights*, Vol. 26, 2015a, pp. 78–87.

———, "Conventional Arms Control in Europe: Some Thoughts About an Uncertain Future," *Deep Cuts Issue Brief*, No. 5, July 2015b.

"Istochnik: v Rossii razrabatyvayut novuyu krylatuyu raketu 'Kalibr-M,'" TASS, January 19, 2019. As of December 19, 2019:
https://tass.ru/armiya-i-opk/5979716

Jervis, Robert, *Perception and Misperception in International Politics*, Princeton, N.J.: Princeton University Press, 1976.

———, "War and Misperception," *Journal of Interdisciplinary History*, Vol. 18, No. 4, Spring 1988, pp. 675–700.

Kofman, Michael, "It's Time to Talk About A2/AD: Rethinking the Russian Military Challenge," *War on the Rocks*, September 5, 2019. As of December 19, 2019:
https://warontherocks.com/2019/09/
its-time-to-talk-about-a2-ad-rethinking-the-russian-military-challenge/

Kühn, Ulrich, "Conventional Arms Control 2.0," *Journal of Slavic Military Studies*, Vol. 26, No. 2, 2013, pp. 189–202.

Kulesa, Łukasz, "The Future of Conventional Arms Control in Europe," *Survival*, Vol. 60, No. 4, 2018, pp. 75–90.

Kulesa, Łukasz, Thomas Frear, and Denitsa Raynova, *Managing Hazardous Incidents in the Euro-Atlantic Area: A New Plan of Action*, London, UK: European Leadership Network, November 2016.

Kuralenko, S. V., "Tendentsii izmeneniya kharaktera vooruzhennoi bor'by v voennykh konfliktakh pervoi poloviny XXI veka," *Voennaya mysl'*, No. 11, 2012.

Lacy, James L., *The Baroque Debate: Public Diplomacy and Naval Arms Control, 1986-1989*, Santa Monica, Calif.: RAND Corporation, N-3121-USDP, 1990a. As of December 26, 2019:
https://www.rand.org/pubs/notes/N3121.html

———, *Naval Arms Control: The Backdrop of History*, Santa Monica, Calif.: RAND Corporation, N-3120-USDP, 1990b. As of December 26, 2019:
https://www.rand.org/pubs/notes/N3120.html

———, *Within and Beyond Naval Confidence-Building: The Legacy and the Options*, Santa Monica, Calif.: RAND Corporation, N-3122-USDP, 1991. As of December 26, 2019:
https://www.rand.org/pubs/notes/N3122.html

Litvinenko, V. I., and I. P. Rusanov, "Osnovnye tendentsii ognevogo porazheniya v sovremennykh operatsiyakh (boevykh deistviyakh)," *Voennaya mysl'*, No. 10, 2014.

Martinho, Lara, *NATO Exercises—Evolution and Lessons Learned*, Brussels, Belgium: Sub-Committee on Future Security and Defence Capabilities, Defence and Security Committee, NATO Parliamentary Assembly, October 13, 2019.

McCausland, Jeffrey D., *The Future of the CFE Treaty: Why It Still Matters*, New York, N.Y.: EastWest Institute, June 2009.

Ministry of Defence of the Republic of Estonia, *National Security Concept 2017*, Tallinn, Estonia, 2017.

Ministry of Defense of the Russian Federation, *Military Doctrine of the Russian Federation*, Moscow, 2014.

———, "Chief of General Staff General of the Army Valery Gerasimov Holds Briefing for Foreign Military Attaches," webpage, December 5, 2018. As of January 17, 2020:
http://eng.mil.ru/en/news_page/country/more.htm?id=12206849@egNews

Ministry of National Defence, *National Threat Assessment 2019*, Vilnius, Lithuania: State Security Department of the Republic of Lithuania, February 5, 2019.

Mizokami, Kyle, "America's Next Cruise Missile Will Strike from 1,000 Miles Away," *Popular Mechanics*, September 12, 2018.

Morris, Lyle J., Michael J. Mazarr, Jeffrey W. Hornung, Stephanie Pezard, Anika Binnendijk, and Marta Kepe, *Gaining Competitive Advantage in the Gray Zone: Response Options for Coercive Aggression Below the Threshold of Major War*, Santa Monica, Calif.: RAND Corporation, RR-2942-OSD, 2019. As of January 9, 2020:
https://www.rand.org/pubs/research_reports/RR2942.html

Norwegian Intelligence Service, *Focus 2019*, Oslo, Norway, February 11, 2019.

Peters, John E., *CFE and Military Stability in Europe*, Santa Monica, Calif.: RAND Corporation, MR-911-OSD, 1997. As of January 17, 2020:
https://www.rand.org/pubs/monograph_reports/MR911.html

Polegaev, V. I., and V. V. Alferov, "O neyadernom sderzhivanii, ego roli i meste v sisteme strategicheskogo sderzhivaniya," *Voennaya mysl'*, No. 7, 2015.

Posen, Barry R., "Crisis Stability and Conventional Arms Control," *Daedalus*, Vol. 120, No. 1, Winter 1991, pp. 217–232.

President of Russia, On the Russian Federation's National Security Strategy, Presidential Edict No. 683, Moscow, December 31, 2015.

———, "Expanded Meeting of the Defense Industry Board," webpage, December 22, 2017. As of January 17, 2020:
https://en.kremlin.ru/events/president/news/56472

———, "Board Meeting of the Ministry of Defense," December 18, 2018.

"Putin Slams 'Aggressive' New US Defence Strategy," *France 24*, December 22, 2017. As of December 27, 2019:
https://www.france24.com/en/20171222-putin-slams-aggressive-new-us-defence-strategy-0

Richter, Wolfgang, *Sub-Regional Arms Control for the Baltics: What is Desirable? What is Feasible?* Deep Cuts Working Paper, No. 8, July 2016.

"Russia Has Resources to Respond to Deployment of New NATO Battalions in Baltics, Poland—Federation Council Member," Interfax, June 15, 2016.

"Russian Flyby of USS Donald Cook in Baltic Sea Alarms Experts," *NBC News*, April 14, 2016.

"Russian Foreign Minister Calls Provocation Plans to Expand Estonia Amari Airfield for NATO Needs," Interfax, October 20, 2015.

"Russian Military Experts Downplay Significance of 'Danger' from Mooted F-22 Europe Deployment," *Gazeta.ru*, August 25, 2015.

Schmidt, Hans-Joachim, *Verified Transparency: New Conceptual Ideas for Conventional Arms Control in Europe*, PRIF Report No. 119, Frankfurt am Main, Germany: Peace Research Institute Frankfurt, 2013.

———, *A Fresh Start of Conventional Arms Control in Europe Will Face Many Structural Problems*, PRIF Report No. 151, Frankfurt am Main, Germany: Peace Research Institute Frankfurt, 2017.

Schulte, Paul, "The Precarious State of Flux of the Conventional Armed Forces in Europe Treaty (CFE)," Carnegie Council for Ethics in International Affairs, June 2, 2011. As of December 20, 2019:
https://www.carnegiecouncil.org/publications/articles_papers_reports/0106

Shakirov, Oleg, *Budushchee Venskogo dokumenta: perspektivy razvitiya mer ukrepleniya doveriya i bezopasnosti v Evrope*, Moscow: Trialog, 2019.

Sivkov, Konstantin, "Nebesnye bastiony," *Voenno-promyshlennyi kur'er*, February 18, 2019.

U.S. Department of Defense and Ministry of National Defense of the People's Republic of China, "Memorandum of Understanding Between the Department of Defense of the United States of America and the Ministry of National Defense of the People's Republic of China Regarding the Rules of Behavior for Safety of Air and Maritime Encounters," Washington, D.C., and Beijing, China, November 9–10, 2014.

U.S. Department of State, *United States Nuclear Risk Reduction Center (NRRC)*, Washington, D.C., 2012. As of December 27, 2019:
https://www.hsdl.org/?view&did=724411

van Ham, Peter, *Modernizing Conventional Arms Control in the Euro-Atlantic Region*, The Hague: Netherlands Institute of International Relations, September 2018.

Vasil'ev, Sergei, and Vladimir Krivoruchko, "Nash nevnyatnyi otvet agressoru," *Voenno-promyshlennyi kur'er*, May 15, 2017.

Vyspasnyak, V. I., A. M. Guralnik, and O. V. Tikhanychev, "Modelirovanie voennykh deistvii: istoriya, sovremennoe sostoyanie i perspektivy razvitiya," *Voennaya mysl'*, No. 7, 2014.

Williams, Ian, "The Russia – NATO A2AD Environment," *Missile Threat*, Center for Strategic and International Studies, January 3, 2017, last modified November 29, 2018. As of December 19, 2019:
https://missilethreat.csis.org/russia-nato-a2ad-environment/

Witkowsky, Anne, Sherman Garnett, and Jeff McCausland, *Salvaging the Conventional Arms Forces in Europe Treaty Regime: Options for Washington*, Brookings Arms Control Series, No. 2, Washington, D.C.: Brookings Institution, March 23, 2010. As of December 20, 2019:
https://www.brookings.edu/wp-content/uploads/2016/06/03_armed_forces_europe_treaty.pdf

Yagolnikov, S. V., "Organizatsiya vozdushno-kosmicheskoi oborony v sovremennykh usloviyakh," *Vestnik AVN*, No. 2, 2016.

Zagorskii, Andrei, "Krizis kontrolya obychnykh vooruzhennykh sil v Evrope—sud'ba Dogovora ob obychnykh vooruzhennykh silakh," in A. Orlov, ed., *Mezhdunarodnye organizatsii i obespechenie mezhdunarodnoi bezopasnosti, Tom 19*, Moscow: Rossiiskoi assotsiatsii mezhdunarodnykh issledovanii, 2009.

Zellner, Wolfgang, "Can This Treaty Be Saved? Breaking the Stalemate on Conventional Forces in Europe," *Arms Control Today*, Vol. 39, No. 7, September 2009, pp. 12–18.

Zellner, Wolfgang, Philip Remler, Wolfgang Richter, Andrei Zagorski, Evgeny P. Buzhinsky, Vladislav L. Chernov, Ali Serdar Erdurmaz, Marc Finaud, Cornelius Friesendorf, P. Terrence Hopmann, Łukasz Kulesa, Igors Rajevs, Benjamin Schaller, Hans-Joachim Schmidt, Niklas Schörning, Oleg Shakirov, and Simon Weiss, *Reducing the Risks of Conventional Deterrence in Europe: Arms Control in the NATO-Russia Contact Zones*, Vienna, Austria: OSCE Network of Think Tanks and Academic Institutions, December 2018.